Straight
And Level

(Growing Up in the '40s)

By Jack Botts

Authors Choice Press
New York   Lincoln   Shanghai

JACK BOTTS is professor emeritus at the University of Nebraska-Lincoln College of Journalism. He was a reporter and editor for 17 years before beginning a 24-year teaching career at Nebraska, where he was sequence head and News-Editorial Department chairman for 18 years.

Straight and Level
(Growing up in the '40s)

All Rights Reserved ©1996, 2002 by Jack Botts

Authors Choice Press
an imprint of iUniverse, Inc.

For information address:
iUniverse
2021 Pine Lake Road, Suite 100
Lincoln, NE 68512
www.iuniverse.com

Originally published by Twin Pines Publishing House (Jack Botts)

ISBN: 0-595-26131-0

Printed in the United States of America

Foreword

These pages grew originally from wanting my children to understand how it was, growing up in a time of war. A generation such as mine, passing directly from high school to military service, probably developed its own brand of thoughts and attitudes. Perhaps we were different from more normally disposed generations because of our unusual experiences, perhaps because we had many experiences. This kind of growing up didn't make us better or more complete, because obviously we missed a lot too. But I think it modified our philosophies and dispositions, and only sometimes for the better. If they succeed, these chapters should reflect the development of those wartime thoughts and attitudes.

I have depended on my memory and my own records, which amount to a casual diary, a brief mission diary and hundreds of letters to my parents and brother. Beyond that I have relied on accounts kept by units, faceless military record keepers and on war historians, many of whom do not agree.

It surprised me to learn that even my diaries and letters, written when I was 18, 19 or 20 years old, turned out to be more accurate and dependable than most "official" records. In fact, in a scale of accuracy I would place official accounts only slightly above my memory of more than 50 years. Such failures in records probably can be traced to bored squadron clerks or, more vitally, to a calculated effort by military organizations to "look good" to historians, even in World War II.

Our fighter pilots, for example, didn't shoot down nearly as many German fighters as the record books claim. Our bombing accuracy, while good enough to help magnificently in winning the war, seldom achieved numbers officially reported. Several works by historians of the air war on the other hand have been superb, despite limitations placed on them by shaky official accounts.

To shore up memory in hazy spots I have called on friends: pilots navigators, bombardiers, flight engineers and gunners, to review or to fill in technical detail. I found that some remember very little and others recall the most trivial events.

It has been impossible to place every minor occurrence precisely in time, but I have included some of the daily humdrum for its tiny part in weaving a fabric of wartime existence. Anyone who studies personal battle experiences in any war, for example, can't help but exclaim at the influence, sometimes the overwhelming presence, of weather.

Many parts of my letters have been omitted because they were personal or insignificant, but the parts printed here are as they were written in the letters.

Finally, because personal accounts of days at war usually produce only a gnat's-eye view, they can leave a reader bewildered: where does this belong in the larger scene? From the first chapters I have tried to keep readers alert to broader developments and to how the pieces fit in the jigsaw.

Jack Botts
Lincoln, NE

Introduction

As I watched a formation of gray crosses flying above and behind us one of them became a yellow-orange flower stamped against brilliant blue sky.

The flower paled quickly into a puff of gray as the other planes left it behind. Only fragments of what had been a B-17 and its crew remained and started to fall.

Shocked, I recoiled defensively a step backward from the gun position and bumped into the open door in the bomb bay bulkhead. Stumbling to the side I sat at the radio desk, tangled in my oxygen hose, heat and interphone lines.

Crumping sounds of close flak bursts turned my eyes to the window inches from my face. Wash from wings and propellers broke up black keyholes of smoke and whipped them away as we plowed through. A sharp rattling sound swept the ship and the left wing outside my window showed an irregular cluster of jagged holes. I pulled my big feet back under the bucket seat.

This must be the war.

It was July 28, 1944. I was a 19-year-old radio operator on my second mission in a B-17 crew. The navigator had just announced by interphone that we would start our bomb run at Ploesti in two minutes.

How, I wondered, had I managed to transport myself from the comfort and security of high school classes in North Dakota to the cramped cold and misery of a bomber 30,000 feet over Romanian oil refineries?

414th Sqdn, 97th B.G. in a little flak at Munich on Oct. 4, 1944.

1. Basic Training

Army basic training in 1943 by its nature didn't differ much from camp to camp. Nevertheless, each recruit couldn't help but hold his own experience exceptional, considering that no ordinary person has suffered in such ways before. An unwritten but ancient rule of military training proclaims new troops beyond the reach of comfort and serenity.

Amarillo Army Air Field in the middle of the Texas panhandle offered bleak possibilities to our straining minds as a couple hundred of us piled off a troop train on June 14, 1943. Blazing sun and swirling dust settled a stifling hand on any enthusiasm we might muster. Before us lay a dreary spread of temporary construction, deposited on a relatively flat part of the desolate breaks between the Canadian and Red rivers.

Each of us marched as well as we could to rows of barracks in breath-stealing heat while balancing two filled bags. Tar paper swathed single-story frame buildings which slouched in tentative alignment on the sand. Wooden duck boards provided connection and direction among the black rows. Beyond hundreds of identical sorry sheds we could identify mess halls, hangars and an airfield control tower.

Two bright looking soldiers appeared in our midst wearing corporals' stripes on uniforms that fit. They recited a roster of about 50 names, including mine, and directed us into one of the squat, plain buildings. They said it would shelter us for the next two months. Assured at least of a temporary home we threw ourselves and our bags on the barren wooden floor.

1

We panted a few minutes, then each of us drew a canvas cot from a nearby storage shed and claimed a satisfactory section of barracks floor for his own. Each reservation included half a window three feet square and a two-foot shelf, complete with a rod for hanging uniforms. To hold the rest of his gear every man drew a regulation Army foot locker which lodged at the foot of his cot.

Now each of us drew a two-inch-thick, cotton-filled mattress, a mattress cover, pillow, two sheets, a pillow case and two OD (olive drab) wool blankets. Our drill instructors, George Ross and Larry O'Brien, ordered us to put the whole mess together. Following prescriptions posted on the inside of a barracks door we stowed our gear in lockers and on shelves.

Our DIs coached as we tangled awkwardly with the cots and tried to assemble presentable beds, or "sacks." They gave us a free afternoon and let us know that we'd discover the real Army the next day. By about 4:30 p.m. we had finished moving in and headed for the latrine for a shower. Somewhat refreshed in the dust and heat, everybody marched off to dinner mess at a big hall across the base. After chow we introduced ourselves and visited with new bunk mates until a recorded taps sounded at nine, sending us thankfully to our cots.

A screeching whistle from our door and brilliant overhead lights brought the Army back to us at five. Our non-coms yelled something about roll call in front of the barracks at six, so we grabbed our towels and kits and stumbled through the darkness to our latrine. Then, shaved and shined, we dressed in fatigues and made up our sacks.

So began a routine that varied for the next two months only in the progress of our basic soldierly instruction. Residents of each barracks marched off to breakfast at five-minute intervals from each squadron. That finished, we began our days of Army lectures, drills and field training designed to shape us into useful manpower.

Ross and O'Brien presented an admirable combination of stern discipline and example, salting that with just enough compassion to make them real. Their success obviously grew from never giving us a moment to weigh the Army's sense or logic.

Air Forces training units like this one even in 1943 had departed in several important ways from standard infantry training. Giving up some purely infantry drill wouldn't disappoint a single man. We'd separate after leaving Amarillo, for example, so we had no reason to train as squads, platoons and companies, etc. We all knew we'd get some kind of specialized training. For organizational purposes the Air Forces called our platoon-size formations "flights" and our company-size complements "squadrons."

We got the usual Army treatment in every other respect. The first morning, after we had to tear our beds apart and remake them Army style, we learned the hand salute and started close-order drill and the manual of arms. In the mornings we usually alternated an hour of marching drill with an hour of lecture on one time-honored Army subject or another, from pitching pup tents to purifying water.

About a week after our arrival we suffered the first installment of a continuing scourge visited upon every serviceman and woman. About six medical orderlies appeared in our squadron and poked syringe needles into our arms as we passed in innocent, forlorn lines. The combination of serums varied somewhat, but every four months or so, no matter our location, we could expect to be scratched or punctured for smallpox, typhoid, tetanus, yellow fever, typhus, cholera and even spotted fever.

After noon mess each day we marched out into the breaks north of the base for field training, which included more marching, much of it double-time, and running the obstacle courses. We spent about an hour a day at physical training or "PT" in which we rolled a lot on the ground. Some brilliant tactician, discovering that an inch of dust covered the calisthenics field, had it sprayed with motor oil about once a week. It transformed the dust into a powdery grime that attached itself to us and our fatigue uniforms.

Fortunately for us our squadron's turn at "PT" came late in the afternoon just before we marched back to the squadron area for showers. We looked like oilfield workers who had fallen in the pits but found a solution in wearing our fatigues into the showers. Brush in one hand and bar of GI soap in the other, we scrubbed under streams of hot water. When we could distinguish skin from cloth we removed that part of the uniform until finally, naked on hands and knees, we finished the daily scrub-down. Our skin scoured to a deep pink, we wrung out our clothes and hung them out to dry. For clotheslines we used about ten slanting guy wires on each side of the barracks, arranged to hold the place down in Texas winds. Standard in neighboring barracks and squadrons, this practice turned the camp each evening into a flock of green geese taking wing.

We alternated each day between the two sets of fatigue uniforms, and within three weeks, instead of deep olive drab they had faded from our scrubbing to a more attractive powder green. Our practiced eyes soon could determine the number of weeks a soldier had been in the Army from the hue of his uniform.

We wore khakis or suntan uniforms only on Saturdays and Sundays as summer "class A" dress, and these, boiled and pressed to a crackling crispness at the camp laundry, also soon turned agreeably lighter. As at most basic training camps we had no pass privileges, but Ross and O'Brien obligingly took our khaki and wool uniforms to an Amarillo tailor who trimmed and tucked them to our measurements. Within a week we had mutated, in appearance at least, from slovenly to soldierly. It helps for a dogface's uniform to stand at attention when he does.

Government-issue shoes presented another problem. Every soldier had two pair. One set resided in precise and brilliant splendor under one's bunk for a week while the other pair tramped the boondocks. At the end of each week their owner by ancient rule had to switch their places.

It confounded us enough to scrub and polish the pair we wore every day for next morning's roll call. But the ingenuity of servicemen, passed on from armies long forgotten, helped us to evade the weekly shoe switch and several other more onerous duties. Every military formation had at least one old timer in its ranks to carry forward these guarded short-cuts.

Mostly they made sense. Who would know, for example, if the pair of shoes under one's bed had not been worn for a month? Our practice became pretty standard: we'd wear one pair for a month or two, cleaning that pair only well enough each evening to pass roll-call inspection before daylight next morning. The pair on display got an armor coat of paste floor wax, casting a glass-like gleam and requiring only a daily swipe for maintenance. Nobody, drill instructors to squadron commander, toppled to our plot. Or perhaps they accepted it as the least painful option.

We stood personal and barracks inspection every Saturday morning before forming up by squadrons on the airfield parking ramps for review by the base commander. We scrubbed our building, floor, walls and windows, put everything in its place, and tightened the blankets on our mattresses. At 9 a.m. we stood at attention, shined, shaved and wearing a crisp uniform, first for our own drill instructors, then for the captain.

The squadron commander's quarter, tossed on a cot here and there, bounced properly, but never raised a whisp of dust. We had learned, again at the knee of our own resident old timer, that a thin film of hair oil applied to each blanket retarded the dust factor for weeks. We also learned that we could button our uniform pocket buttons permanently by cutting them off and sewing them onto the button holes in the flaps. Any solemn regard among us for Army rules had dimmed almost to invisibility within weeks.

Two of us once managed to avoid Saturday morning review, which in the Texas summer heat imposed pain almost beyond endurance. Each week we marched by squadrons onto that frying hot concrete, there to stand it seemed until death or war's end intervened. Every non-com and officer with a voice had to "report" in unbroken succession while we in airless formations felt our heels, knees and hipbones fuse to aching stone. Perspiration crept ever lower until it filled leggings and shoes. We held it an article of faith that we would hear the call finally to "march in review" only after an acceptable number of us had passed out.

The two of us noticed that Ross and O'Brien counted us and took roll for those reviews before we marched away from our barracks. We also noted that our formation and all others stood for several minutes in the hangar area waiting to take their proper positions before marching onto the improvised parade grounds. One Saturday we both slipped off the end of our formation, walked through a hangar and back to the Post Exchange for an early beer. We didn't worry about being recognized in a crowd of thousands--all dressed in khakis. Ross' report that day that we were "all present and accounted for" wasn't quite true.

Cpls. Ross and O'Brien

2. War for a Teenager

Every healthy young American male in the early '40s knew he was headed into military service. The art came in putting a providential spin on the matter.

World War II had started without me as it had for most Americans. When Hitler sent his armies into Poland in September of 1939 I wasn't quite 15 years old and had barely started my sophomore year at Oakes high school in North Dakota. My concerns until then focused on my acne and whether my 110 pounds and scarecrow build made it sensible to try for the football team. Anyway, it turned out that we had enough war to go around.

Its battles invaded our lives in North Dakota that fall, not brutally as in Europe, but with subtle, cold impressions of excitement and foreboding. Youth felt the seduction that goes with all wars. Parents and others with age and wisdom worried as they had in all wars.

We pored over Life Magazine's maps and accounts after British cruisers fought the German pocket battleship Graf Spee off the River Plate late in 1939. After Poland fell and during the quiet winter of 1939-1940, high school students in Oakes, as everywhere, fed our curiosities. In our group we didn't talk much of fighting someday ourselves but it must have entered our minds.

When Hitler in May, 1940, turned a watching war into one of blitzkreig our interest grew even more intense.

We lived on battle information along with our chemistry and geometry, and if we leaned toward a particular aspect of warfare it was to air battles, the planes and the men in them. Through the summer of 1940 and the next winter we followed the great air event that became in history the Battle of Britain. From radio accounts and from our reading we lived with Hurricane and Spitfire pilots who rose in the air each few hours to defend their land against Heinkels, Junkers and Messerschmitts. Hope and despair grew for us in alternating surges.

Our graduation was still a year away when Germany invaded the Soviet Union in June, 1941. We all listened and read intently as the Wehrmacht swept everything before it through the summer and fall of its last blitz. About the time German armies discovered in the cold that the Soviet Union was a tough chew, Japanese naval and air forces struck Pearl Harbor. And so our country entered the war which, with all its pain and consequences, filled our lives for nearly three and a half years. Back in the spring of 1942 dedication paced each day until our graduation, until we became real.

Some older students joined the National Guard, hoping to gain time and training before being shipped to battle areas. They were, in fact, first to go overseas. One of my best high school friends in a fit of eagerness only he could muster inquired about joining the Royal Canadian Air Force. No problem, he learned. Sure, we could join at 17 and didn't even need parental approval, but the RCAF made U.S. volunteers give up their citizenship. Neither of us had much to say about it, and the subject never surfaced again.

Graduation from high school in May of 1942 aligned us almost perfectly with the draft. In this position we'd have been abnormal for the times if we hadn't studied ways to gain some advantage over the system. Few tried to beat conscription, but we wanted to avoid a direct shunt into the infantry. All kinds of alternatives presented themselves, and although several of us had a cushion between graduation and our 18th birthdays, we examined every option, including enlistment.

That last choice got brief consideration once we compared notes and discovered that enlistment seemed to short-circuit the enlistee into the worst possible assignments. My disdain for ground or sea duty in the ranks partly fed my search for an option. My brother John, two and a half years older than I and feeling the national service draft breathing warm on his neck, shared and stimulated my interest.

My graduation day passed in May just a few days after our troops surrendered the Philippines to Japanese invaders. We all seemed to hang between childhood and full manhood, doped with nervous hope and apprehension. Some time in July brother John and I learned about a Signal Corps program that allowed qualified men to attend college classes in electronics before being inducted for active duty. Military services then needed men who understood high frequency techniques and especially radar, the new, wonderful and too often mysterious electronic tool. The program had no visible connection with planes or flying--my only disappointment.

We wrote for more information and soon took a government exam. A letter told us we'd begin our training in August at the State School of Science in Wahpeton, only about 80 miles away. Not quite 18, I started classes with the buoyant self-assurance of valuable education before being drafted. Everything pointed to Army Signal Corps duty for me, eventually.

Little of this stirred my silly brain to serious concentration in the fall of 1942. Excitement over the unknown nourishes both mind and body at the age of 17.

The government, specifically the Seventh Service Command, had contracted with the School of Science to provide instruction for about 60 at the start. Each of us Signal Corps students, called Assistant Technician Trainees, received a monthly check for $94. Far more than I had ever earned, it brightened my days. Every three months instructors decided whether we remained in training, were called up or returned home to await the draft. Three of these three-month training sessions constituted the entire program. Classes included math, radio theory and labs. Except for staggering bouts with higher math I got along well.

We started these classes at about the time our Marines landed on the island of Guadalcanal in the Solomons, the first major allied offensive of the Pacific war. Canadian and British forces had failed in an assault on the French port of Dieppe. Small units of U.S. heavy bombers that summer and fall made their first tentative daylight thrusts against the Third Reich.

Early in November we advanced to the second three-month phase. Subjects made greater demands on our poor intellects, but those of us who had survived put our heads down in determination. We began to use more real equipment in our labs, applying more complex theory to circuits as we used them.

Twenty of us transferred on Feb. 1, 1943, to Grand Forks, where we would complete our final three months of training at the University of North Dakota. At the same time the government raised our pay to $135 a month. Grand Forks' better restaurants and entertainment made up for its bitter cold and snowstorms.

There I received notice to report for physical examination. Jokes about induction, while still tempered by the unknown, now displayed a touch of arrogance. This physical couldn't have detected any but the most obvious defects, and those of us in line for examination even kidded the doctors about their "warm body" approach. Local Draft Board No.1, Dickey County, N.D., classified me 1-A on March 27.

Our instructors and their demands, meanwhile, grew noticeably tougher. We swore daily during those last three months that calculus would end our lives prematurely and that we were much too young and tender for that line of work. While solving most problems I vowed that should I survive to war's end I'd never again take up pencil seriously in mathematical pursuit.

After our classes ended we caught a bus home and within days my brother received notice to report for active Army duty. I had a whole week or 10 days of carefree abandon before receiving the official "Order to Report for Induction."

On May 24, 1943, eleven of us, including Maynard Furan, a high school friend, boarded a train to Ft. Snelling, Minn., near Minneapolis. That night we bedded down in our first Army barracks.

Nobody ever forgets his or her military induction, standard and uneventful though it usually is. We all managed a facade of solemnity, but our thoughts drifted to other matters, such as: "What happens next?" The words "to protect and defend" our country carried implications none of us had completely examined on May 27, 1943.

Army doctors explored our bodies and minds for a couple of days at their convenience and our discomfort. We struggled through a long intelligence quiz which helped our testers to decide where and how we could serve our country best.

These service tests and decisions based on them during several wars have stirred servicemen to uncontrolled mirth. None of my fellow inductees had much faith in the process, and indeed considered the words logic and military administration contradictory. I still clung to a hope that somebody would note my expensive electronic training by the Signal Corps.

The Army now sent us home for a few days, presumably to settle our affairs and say goodby. That done, we headed back to Snelling. On the train to Minneapolis Maynard and I smoked a couple of cigars, proving to the watching world that we had passed into manhood, and proving to ourselves that we still had a way to go. Our appetites, even our breathing, betrayed us for days.

Now a part of that great organized force called the Army of the United States, we drew our uniforms: summer and winter dress, fatigue twills, underwear, socks, shoes, shaving kit, towels, helmet liner, web belt, canteen, mess kit, raincoat, leggings, gas mask and two barracks bags. We all packed our "civvies" and sent them home. Starting with our identification, our "dog" tags, we tried everything on. Every face exposed its owner's disappointment. New uniforms never fit. It's unwritten Army and Navy law that recruits must appear to have been dressed at a rummage sale.

Riding street cars we visited friends in Minneapolis who kidded us about those new shaving kits. Our struggling beards would develop, surely, so we said something about keeping the kits to throw at the Germans or Japanese. Our appearance in those rumpled and ill-fitting khakis could not have instilled much confidence in us as defenders of the Western World.

Guard duty one rainy night at Snelling was a four-hour event calculated more to initiate me into Army ways than to protect the old fort. It was only the first of many miseries in my service career peculiar to tall people. My short raincoat allowed rainwater to drain directly into the tops of my leggings and from there into my shoes.

We formed up a few times and marched off awkwardly to latrine or kitchen duty, but spent most of these few days at the induction center in interviews. Again jokes and speculation grew about how poorly the Army would match our talents and training with its needs.

About 4 p.m. one day early in June our assignments finally appeared on a bulletin board and we crowded close to learn our fates. Those in charge had posted me to the Army Air Forces for basic training at Amarillo, Texas. This surpassed the Signal Corps in my view, although such an assignment seemed out of bounds because of my training. The Army directed Maynard to an infantry basic training camp in the South, a fate we had tried so desperately to avoid.

We joked nervously about tomorrows we couldn't comprehend and wished each other well. Next morning, on June 13, after hurried packing and a handshake, we went to our separate trains. Our paths never crossed again until war's end.

Eleven of us from Dickey County draft. Author at left, Maynard Furan at his left.

Local Board No.
Stony County   051
APR 22 1943   051
Ellendale, N. Dak.

(Local Board Date Stamp With Code)

ORDER TO REPORT FOR INDUCTION

The President of the United States,

To _____ Jack _____ C _____ _____
      (First name)   (Middle name)   (Last name)

Order No. ___ 10,782 ___

GREETING:

Having submitted yourself to a local board composed of your neighbors for the purpose of determining your availability for training and service in the land or naval forces of the United States, you are hereby notified that you have now been selected for training and service therein.

You will, therefore, report to the local board named above at _____
Ellendale, N. Dak. (Place of reporting)

at _6:00_ A. m., on the _24th_ day of _____ May _____ 19__43__
(Hour of reporting)

This local board will furnish transportation to an induction station. You will there be examined, and, if accepted for training and service, you will then be inducted into the land or naval forces.

Persons reporting to the induction station in some instances may be rejected for physical or other reasons. It is well to keep this in mind in arranging your affairs, to prevent any undue hardship if you are rejected at the induction station. If you are employed, you should explain your employer of this notice and of the possibility that you may not be accepted at the induction station. Your employer can then be prepared to replace you if you are accepted, or to continue your employment if you are rejected.

Willful failure to report promptly to this local board at the hour and on the day named in this notice is a violation of the Selective Training and Service Act of 1940, as amended, and subjects the violator to fine and imprisonment.

If you are so far removed from your own local board that reporting in compliance with this order will be a serious hardship and you desire to report to a local board in the area of which you are now located, go immediately to that local board and make written request for transfer of your delivery for induction, taking this order with you.

Elmer J. Anthe (signature)

Member and clerk of the local board

D. S. S. Form 150
(Revised 1-15-43)

NOTICE OF CLASSIFICATION

Jack _____ Chester _____ Scott
(First name)   (Middle name)   (Last name)

Order No. _10,782_ has been classified in Class __1-A__

(Until _____, 19____)
(Insert date for Class II-A and II-B only)

by ☒ Local Board.
    ☐ Board of Appeal (by vote of _____ to _____).
    ☐ President.

March 27 19_43_
(Date of mailing)   (Member of local board)

The law requires you, subject to heavy penalty for violation, to have this notice, in addition to your Registration Certificate (Form 2), in your personal possession at all times—to exhibit it upon request to authorized officials—to surrender it, upon entering the armed forces, to your commanding officer.

DSS Form 57. (Rev. 11-16-42)

(Cut along this line)

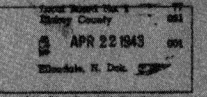

3. Serious Drilling

Five days a week we drilled, usually under the eyes and commands of our own drill instructors, but sometimes under alleged experts. We threw dummy grenades. We ran through chambers of tear gas to test our use of the gas masks. We fired the Enfield rifle for practice and for record. Then we fired 45 cal. revolvers and Thompson machine guns for record. Because of all the noise we marched back from the firing range each night deaf to all commands for the first mile or two.

We spent three evenings after chow cleaning the cosmoline from those Enfields which had been in cases since World War I. Never a satisfactory rifle even when new, they served us well as training arms, perhaps, but drew considerable scorn from those who had to carry or fire them. For sidearms practice we didn't use the Colt 45 automatic, but British-made Webley 45 revolvers so worn their cylinders wouldn't hold a load of ammunition without help.

For troops not in the least interested in rifle marksmanship we did fairly well, about six in our flight gaining Sharpshooter designation. We all enjoyed firing the Thompsons, which we considered a good weapon. As with the rifles, however, we couldn't even guess why we needed practice with them. With pistols, the only weapon we would ever carry, we were hopeless. Might as well throw the thing at the enemy, we thought.

I remember that firing range only because of its location. Some marvel in planning, probably a brother to the person who designed my raincoat, placed it in one of the dry ravines north of the base. Dry, that is, until it rained. Great gouts of water came crashing through it on one August day during what can only be called a Texas-size rainstorm. We had fired earlier in the day and stood thankfully in our showers when we heard about two flights who had to scramble for their lives up the sides of the ravine. Rumors said several had drowned, but we heard no official report.

That rainstorm carried away all the duckboards in camp so we spent the next day finding them, piled by the hundreds in another ravine, and staking them down where they belonged. It rained that day too, and the next, so we all slithered about in our raincoats, trying to stay free of mud, if not entirely dry. We had by now scrubbed our shoes in the showers so often that they had taken the characteristics of cast iron. Cpl. Ross requisitioned a tin of leather oil, but it didn't help much.

I respected and liked our two corporals and got along fine with most non-coms in the orderly room, including a master sergeant named Casa. I failed somehow to impress the squadron first sergeant, however, and he caused me hardship beyond description. At one point in every day's drilling this fellow without fail braced our flight for an impromptu inspection. My failures in his mind may have been manifold, but he pounced on the top button of my fatigue uniform as an object for his wrath.

"Unbutton it, soldier!"

He carried a baton, as a colonel of artillery might, and with it always tapped that button as he screamed the order. I yelped in return, and at each confrontation explained that a little triangle on my chest had been sunburned

16

raw. A base fight surgeon had given me some salve for it and told me to button my top button.

My explanation only infuriated this first soldier, whose name, I swear, was Grinder. He clearly placed himself above any silly medic. He towered above me and, peering down his skinny nose, repeated his order as I stared into his necktie. For about a week I repeated this scene, unbuttoning for Grinder, then buttoning up again once our flight had marched away. I saved myself eventually only in learning to watch for him and to unfasten that button when he appeared within range. My peripheral vision improved all summer.

Our barracks, or flight, consisted in almost equal numbers of draftees from Texas on one side of the aisle and from North Dakota and Minnesota on the other. Nearly all of us were 18, except for three or four Texans in their 30s who apparently had enjoyed deferments. We talked for hours during the evenings and given the difference in geographical backgrounds, merged fairly well. We threw the usual good natured insults at each other but, perhaps because of our temporary association, survived without serious problems.

Soon after our arrival we got orders to memorize our General Orders, having to do mostly with how a soldier conducts himself during guard duty. Given printed copies and a deadline we recited them to each other for days. When we discovered two non-readers in our midst the rest of us pitched in as teachers. To our credit everybody passed the oral test.

Close-order drill holds the average inductee's interest about half an hour. After that, listening to orders while marching requires a strength of will not always found in an 18-year-old. The military's answer to that from prehistoric times has been to condition one's response by repetition. We soon learned to hear and react to commands automatically, often while thinking of other things. The Army accepted that and demonstrated daily that it wasn't much interested in our thoughts.

Its standards didn't allow for bobbing up and down while marching, however, and two boys, one from Texas and one from North Dakota, in many of their evening hours practiced ways to un-bob their gaits.

Most of us gained weight, even in all that heat. We expected it. Constant demands on our muscles, combined with piles of bulky and rich food, put most of us in better physical shape than before we belonged to Uncle Sam.

Our mess halls turned out a grist that while not always attractive, filled our bellies. I nearly always found Army food acceptable, even during basic training, and didn't dwell much on finer points of its preparation or display. Many others gave up on it when they could and went to the Post Exchange for a hamburger. Except for Sunday evenings, however, we couldn't do that in basic training. We marched to chow for all three meals a day and marched back again.

Once, during field exercises in our last few weeks at Amarillo, some of us ate well. We had gone into the breaks between the base and the Canadian River, mostly to see if we could carry packs through miles of rough country. Told to fall out at about 5 p.m., we looked for places to pitch our pup tents. A mess orderly wheeled up in a Jeep and asked if anyone in our flight could cut up a quarter of beef. Having learned a little meat cutting from my dad in the family store, I got in beside him.

A mess truck crew had dumped our squadron chow in an open area. A corporal and three orderlies had pulled things together pretty well and set up a field kitchen. They had a meat saw and a couple of knives but none of them had cut up a beef before. The quarter, sewed in burlap, shouldn't cause problems, I told the corporal, especially if he could provide an incentive for my work, say a handful of steaks. He agreed, and in half an hour his beef quarter had turned into usable segments. Four of us made our own fire that night and fried some very tasty steaks on the bottoms of our mess kits. The rest had stew, and not until about 9 o'clock, so it paid for once to defy the old soldier's motto: never volunteer.

Each of us drew assignment to kitchen police, or mess duty, once every three weeks and latrine duty once every ten days. Three recruits could clean a latrine in four hours, from lights out at 9 p.m. to 1 a.m., but the woes of K.P. kept us busy for about 10 hours each time.

The depth of our miseries depended entirely on how the mess sergeant assigned us. Duties always involved scrubbing something within an inch of its life, but we found the coffee detail almost enjoyable. Required only to keep three 10-gallon drip machines going, one even had time to visit with other unfortunates on the chow line.

We dreaded with passion any assignment to pots and pans. Ten- and 15-gallon aluminum pots used in food preparation often needed washing and scrubbing half a dozen times a day. Frying and baking pans required chisels to free crusts of burned food and grease. Hundred-plus temperatures and scalding water left us limp and barely pulsating after 10 hours.

Such wretchedness easily causes aberrant behavior, which could explain our singing, but that clearly grew from another time-honored Army plot. We sang in formations and we sang as we dug latrine ditches. We sang on K.P. and we sang as we gathered our fatigues from improvised lines. Not well, mind you, but the kind of barracks-room bawling heard in all armies for centuries. We sang any tune that came to mind, from "I've Got Sixpence" to the latest hit from Broadway. It needed only someone in the crowd to start and we were off. This homely miracle of sound seemed to appease our souls, and we had the Army's blessing.

What serviceman or woman from the 40s doesn't remember those ditties about their chow:

>*"Oh the coffee that they feed us*
>*They say is mighty fine.*
>*It's good for cuts and bruises*
>*And tastes like iodine.*
>*Oh I don't want no more of Army life;*
>*Gee, Mom, I want to go home.*
>
>*Oh the biscuits that they feed us*
>*They say are mighty fine.*
>*One fell off the table*
>*And killed a pal of mine.*
>*Gee, Mom, I want to go home."*

In the middle of July, about the time our troops invaded Sicily, interviewers held us captive in little cubicles for several hours at a time. They obviously sought an Army Air Forces niche for each of us. During my third session a mousy-faced lieutenant discovered in my file that I had attended high frequency radio school for nine months. He visibly leaped at the possibilities. I still remember his words:

"How would you like to be in a bomber crew?"

It sounded just fine to me, I told him.

He told me that the Air Forces needed radiomen for bomber crews and I fit the requirements.

He said I qualified for officer training as a pilot, but added discouragingly that the Army washed out about 80 percent of pilot trainees at that time. He advised me to take advantage of my radio background and go for crew training.

His argument made sense then, but it had allowed a fine opportunity to pass. At least if I had no aptitude as a pilot, crew training still remained, probably as a radio operator. This lieutenant performed his duty, surely, but couldn't know how well any of us might do.

Our plague of training ran its hot and dreary course. We grew harder and soaked up useful service trivia, but we also grew impatient with a tiresome and predictable schedule. Some of us sought refuge in our free time scrambling through several early model B-17s parked on hangar ramps. Flight engineers being trained at Amarillo used the Seventeens for part of their classes. Sitting at the radio operator's desk in one of them one couldn't help wondering what lay ahead.

We "graduated" from basic in the middle of August and on the 18th, the day after our troops took Sicily, packed to move on. Our postings, tacked to our barracks door, announced that four of us in our flight would go to the Army Air Forces Technical School at Sioux Falls, S.D., for training as radiomen. A few headed for flight mechanics' schools and a greater number to gunnery schools. A few unfortunates held orders to cooks school and others went into transportation forces, which meant truck driving.

Interest levels surged anew. Again the unknown drew us into its tantalizing embrace as we struggled with our bags on the way to trains and unfamiliar places.

4. Radio School

Sioux Falls Army Air Forces Technical School had real asphalt streets for each squadron. Shallow ditches about four feet wide separated the streets from rows of tarpaper-covered barracks. A north-south row of white frame buildings, each a good 200 feet by 50 feet, divided the base into two sections. We learned as we arrived that we would attend radio classes in these white structures.

About 80 of us on Aug. 20, 1943, settled into a barracks similar to the Amarillo buildings except for having a concrete floor and three coal-fired space heaters in the middle aisle. Instead of canvas cots we now slept in double-deck wooden bunks with real springs and a cotton mattress three inches thick. Sheer ecstasy after basic training.

We learned that 18 weeks of bomber crew radio instruction lay ahead of us. At the end of each week, if we survived the tests, we'd graduate to another phase in another building. We started our movable feast of classes in the northernmost classroom, advancing one building southward each week.

Three new barracks or flights like ours formed a class. Each of those three flights took a third of the day, or an eight-hour shift in the classroom. Once a month we'd change shifts. A model of efficiency, to be sure, but the Training Command displayed little regard for the wear and tear on those of us trying to fit into its patterns.

Despite a sheaf of irritating rules and constrictions which always raised bitter complaints among trainees, one can't help but admire the planning that managed to fit service training and weapons production into wartime military needs. After 1942, especially, evidence of poor planning gradually diminished. Bought partly by our sweat and frustration, this smoothly running machine had few admirers at the time.

Part of our pattern included an hour of PT every week day and regular stints at latrine and KP duty. We could get one 12-hour pass to town every weekend and on occasion a two-day pass. These appeared promising to us when we arrived, but someone pointed out that the base held 40,000 of us, just about the same number as the population in town. One dim viewer cracked that in order to get a pass we'd have to arrange for some citizen to leave town.

We tried the PX on our side of the base and the first night filled up on local beer which wasn't remotely related to the 3.2 suds we had swilled in Texas. A friend, named Burge, from my Amarillo days discovered that strong brew didn't team well with a top bunk. Not used to either, he fell to the concrete floor during the night and broke his shoulder. Some of us visited him in the base hospital a few days later and learned that his injury would win him a discharge as soon as it mended. Despite his pain he said he'd do it all over again for a pass back home.

My first classes duplicated theories and exercises I had completed in Wahpeton a year before. Our instructor sent me to a major in charge of instruction who pulled out my training folder and agreed that nearly three months of classes at Sioux Falls would repeat my earlier work. I jumped at his proposal to allow me to take the weekly tests in succession until I encountered new material, which probably would be bomber equipment. That afternoon the school examiners, called "Quiz Kids," in a few hours passed me along to the 11th week.

My only problem came in International Morse Code, required of airborne radio operators. Before joining the 11th week class I'd spend several weeks in the code rooms. Radio trainees normally spent half a day at learning code. Eight hours a day clamped in earphones didn't sound appealing to me, but it had been my choice.

Ham radio operators taught us code, and very well. Four weeks with them passed quickly but amounted to life in an eerie tunnel. I felt the presence of earphones even in my bunk. Dits and dahs filled every waking moment until patient teachers, obviously tired of my presence, decided to kick me ahead to the advanced class.

I regretted leaving my original bunch, especially those who had come up with me from Amarillo, and moved across the base with some apprehension to a flight just starting its 11th week. Empty bunks in this barracks proved that not everyone had passed the weekly tests. A ticket to gunnery school awaited those who flunked.

Allied troops had invaded Italy during my code room days. Soviet armies had pushed across the Dnieper and our forces had squeezed the Japanese out of the Solomons. My new radio class entered the equipment phase of our training with a feeling that the war, while a long way from over, was going our way. In our casual minutes we sang or whistled tunes from "Oklahoma!"

We studied in succession Air Forces radio command and liaison sets, the radio compass, blind landing and radar identification equipment. Some, like the SCR 274 Command set and the SCR 287 high-powered liaison set, had been in Signal Corps use for many years. The very high frequency

24

(VHF) SCR 522 command set and the SCR 269 radio compass had come from air war requirements.

Every heavy bomber carried 11 separate pieces of radio equipment, but some, like the instrument approach system, for blind landings, marker beacon receivers, radar IFF and all antenna systems required only regular inspection by a radio operator. If our hardware broke down or became damaged in flight and couldn't be fixed on the spot, we filled out an unsatisfactory report form to aid ground crewmen.

My first stripe, or advance in rank, came at Sioux Falls, only because the Table of Organization specified Private First Class rank for anyone attending a technical school. It meant a few bucks raise in pay from the $40 a month for privates. We all saluted each other in fun but felt about the same. We sat for hours in our bunks sewing those little chevrons and the radio operator's triangular patch to our shirt and blouse sleeves.

Bob Henry, a hometown friend, had arrived for training. I visited him in his barracks one Saturday and found a room full of dispirited and cynical men. Having flunked out of pilot training he and his friends had nothing but sarcastic remarks about their new prospects. He considered me foolish to have hastened my training because he saw air crews as nothing but cannon fodder. He apparently didn't understand that air crews included pilots.

Those in my barracks believed in their work. We piled into our assignments and lab work as if the war depended on us. Classes in August and September turned into a drag because we had night shifts and couldn't sleep well in the daytime heat and light, but we considered it only an inconvenience.

Weekend passes to town brightened our lives, even if we had to fight crowds of GIs everywhere. Our hair had to measure less than an inch long before we could pass the front gate, but now, at least, we could hire a civilian barber. Two or three Sioux Falls movie houses offered a better fare than our base theaters, and in good weather we enjoyed some nice parks.

No matter which shift we might be assigned we still had to march off to an hour of PT every day. Our trainers had us run a half-mile track for most of that hour, grunting and complaining all the way. When bone-chilling weather came to southeast South Dakota our forced running put several trainees in the post infirmary with pneumonia. The officer in charge of our PT abruptly disappeared from that job, but we guessed that he'd probably cause pain for GIs wherever he landed.

We didn't stand weekly review here, but a 9 a.m. inspection on Saturday mornings kept us up on Friday nights, scrubbing the barracks floor and shaking dust out of our blankets. When temperatures went off the bottom of the scale in December and January our scrubbing water turned to ice on the barracks floor except for about eight feet around each stove.

When it turned cold we set up a scheduled "fire watch" in each barracks. For eight-hour periods each of us took turns at keeping the stoves stoked with coal, which we hauled from bins on the outside. Those of us sleeping on top bunks needed no blankets at all and those on the bottom piled everything they owned on their beds to stay warm.

We complained bitterly at the Training Command's absurd practice of specifying the uniform of the day according to daily changes in the weather. A system of flags displayed over each squadron orderly room told us what to wear, and woe unto the poor slob who didn't look before getting dressed. Worst of all, our dress for cold, rainy or snowy weather included the helmet liner. We detested that plastic pot, especially during visits to town. Besides being uncomfortable, those awkward liners made a busload of trainees look like a truckload of watermelon.

My dad arrived by bus for a visit one weekend in September. We had to share a hotel room with another trainee and his father. I'm sure Dad wanted to see how his 18-year-old son had survived his first months in the Army. We spent about a day and a half walking and talking. Around my 19th birthday in October my mom arrived for a similar weekend, and was filled with assurances that her son had his share of food and care.

On Oct. 14 the Eighth Air Force lost 60 B17s in a raid against Schweinfurt. On Oct. 22, our Combined Chiefs of Staff agreed to establish the Fifteenth Air Force in the Mediterranean, a move later to influence my part of the war.

We all passed our required 35 words-per-minute in the code rooms by the 14th week. At that point we dropped code classes and practiced using Air Forces equipment all day. We sent and received messages on the three two-way sets, and we plotted positions using the radio compass.

On Dec. 20 the 97th Bomb Group, my combat "outfit" a few months later, moved from Tunisia to Italy.

Those in my class spent about three days sending messages to each other by flashing Aldis lamp signals between towers that stood at each corner of the base. Then instructors put us in simulated bomber radio rooms where, following Army Air Forces signal operating instructions, we communicated with our "base." Not quite authentic, these mock-ups should have registered about 50 below zero.

We fired recognition flare guns, learned our radio "Q" signals, plotted our positions from bearings given us by radio and learned the essentials of cryptographic bomber

27

and weather codes. We mastered the phonetic alphabet for voice communication, giving us an excuse to practice the "Roger dodger, over and out" jargon even in the barracks or in town. Hot shots, to be sure.

A few of our instructors in this phase had flown at least 25 missions in Europe. We regarded them with awe, and their presence made sense. When they told us that mastering a machine or procedure might save our lives, we listened. We learned that the first bomb crews sent to the Pacific or to Europe in 1942 lacked both technical and gunnery training. Much of our instruction, they told us, came directly from lessons they had to learn on the job. It didn't reassure us much, however, to note that most of them wore the Purple Heart ribbon.

During the last week of instruction we went into the "wild blue yonder." Planes at the base included a couple of old Curtiss Owls and half a dozen Piper observation types. They carried us aloft individually for about an hour at a time, riding in the back seat behind a pilot.. We wore earphones attached to a small receiver, and a clipboard on the lap held a radio log and sending key that plugged into a small transmitter. We sent coded messages to our base operator and received similar dispatches from him.

All this was rudimentary, certainly, but enough to help somebody decide whether we could--or couldn't--carry out basic communication functions under cramped and awkward conditions. I looked back at this exercise later convinced that it came close to real circumstances only in the temperature. A bone-chilling cold spell this last week in December made an unheated light plane pretty frosty. After only an hour we could scarcely untangle our brittle bodies from the narrow seat.

After a final series of tests we graduated as Radio Operator-Mechanics, giving us a Tech Order designation that also brought us Corporals' stripes and a pair of silver air crew wings. The ceremony and wings impressed me and others as intended. We now held a station at least a touch exalted in our minds. Not a few of us spent the first evening burnishing those winged emblems to a fine sheen.

What next? We knew that gunnery school followed in our training sequence, but where? As we completed our classes, President Roosevelt, Britain's Prime Minister Churchill and China's President Chiang Kai-shek had met in Cairo to plan the rest of our wartime course. One of their decisions appointed a theater commander for my European career: Gen. Dwight Eisenhower.

We got our expecterd postings soon after the first of the new year. Nearly all in my class boarded a troop train on Jan. 4, 1944, bound for a new gunnery school in Yuma, Arizona. We knew we wouldn't miss South Dakota's chill, but none of us under all his proud bluster could forecast what the winds of destiny might blow his way. Whatever came, we felt only somewhat more prepared to meet it.

5. Troop Trains

Wartime troop trains like this one to Yuma functioned only to carry large numbers of service people, feeding and bedding them enroute. Throwing such crowds into restricted quarters for several days at a time couldn't fail to confound principles of hygiene and privacy. Poor souls sentenced to them arrived at destinations battered, soiled and stunned.

Transportation commands had pressed into service hundreds of retired coaches from remote sidings, apparently not pausing even to clean them. But cars for troop trains, the kind we found new ways to loathe, had been mail or baggage carriers before their reincarnation for the military.

Steel pipes arranged in sets from floor to ceiling supported three frames on which canvas cots stretched one above the other and perpendicular to the side of the car. A three-foot aisle provided passage along one side. Each set of pipes allowed scarcely room for a captive traveler to mount or dismount from his cot. Vertical space limitations prevented sitting on the canvas. One escaped this infernal rack only by standing or, if fortunate, finding space on the aisle floor to sit.

Each train included a mess car, not usually placed in the middle as reason might dictate, but at one end. This forced most tired and hungry GIs to step over or past hundreds of others while carrying a mess kit of hot chow and a pint of boiling coffee. Because of the numbers to be fed, a frantic lurching, dripping and cursing continued through most daylight hours, aggravated regularly by poor roadbeds and unexpected stops.

To clean or relieve himself one stood in another line waiting for a free washbasin and toilet, either of which in such conditions offered layers of filth and a dizzying stench. Someone sarcastically suggested distilling the essence of our trip into a perfume to be sent to our enemies. He would call it "Three Days on a Troop Train."

We raised a standing prayer that the great god of transportation might strike off a special medal for anyone enduring this test. What horrors of combat still to come, we asked ourselves, could exceed these on the rails.

Once every day the trainmaster halted our progress, probably to gain open space and a breath of freshness himself. Ordered to disembark for calisthenics and giddy from foul air and exhaustion, we welcomed weeds and cinders of the right-of-way. No amount of threatening or pleading could enlist us into formal exercise. We sought only to breathe and stare at the sky.

When at last this machine from Hell dropped us along a siding near Yuma on January 7 we piled out of cars to look for our bags. Instead of eager young men we gave the appearance of creatures from space, condemned to an exile of aimless wandering. Having extracted our barracks bags from a pile we threw them and ourselves on trucks which carted us to our new base and, we hoped, clean showers and uniforms.

6. Gunnery School

We had arrived at an aerial gunnery school in the making. Tents, piles of lumber and packing cases bordered one side of the new airfield north of Yuma. Our class moved into rows of six-man tents built on wooden floors.

Within days we started instruction, the fourth class to begin in as many weeks. Within two weeks of our arrival construction crews had completed several rows of frame barracks, a mess hall and a classroom. Emergency construction under wartime priorities had created a school out of a desert. Even the sand, planted, fertilized and irrigated, sprouted into acres of grass around the new buildings.

The 50 Cal. Browning M2 machine gun in all its airborne applications became our center of attention for six weeks. We grew to value, if not love, this gun, so critical to our survival. Standardized by the services as far back as 1930, it had been honed and tuned to an effective and reliable weapon.

The Browning had a muzzle velocity of 2,800 feet per second. Those in the Army Air Forces, using a pneumatic buffer and helical recoil springs, had increased their cyclic rate from 800 to 1100 rounds per minute. That didn't mean a gunner could fire it for a minute without stopping. Even barrels exposed to sub-zero cold air turned red hot unless the shooter weaned them to 10- or 20-round bursts.

In classrooms we learned all the parts and mastered disassembling and assembling the gun, even in the dark. But we couldn't fire it--yet. Our jaws dropped in disbelief one morning during the first week when instructors handed each of us a Winchester Model 12 pump-action shotgun.

We started shooting these at clay pigeons, loosed at various angles from trap houses, high and low. Our shotguns had post and ring sights, much like the post-mounted machine guns, and we learned to lead our clay targets in radiuses of the ring, depending on the angle each target took in its flight. After the first morning on the skeet range our shoulders, aching from hundreds of recoils, wouldn't even permit a salute.

During the second week we fired from 50-foot towers at clay disks coming at us from below. Because we had to fire faster in the towers we used Remington semi-automatic shotguns which lacked compensators on their muzzles. After only a few rounds our shoulders and arms started swelling in protest, so most of us stuffed towels inside the shoulders of our coveralls.

In two weeks we mastered the murder of clay disks from a fixed position and our instructors put us in motion as well as our targets. Each of us in turn stood on the bed of a pickup truck, supported only by a three-foot ring of pipe at about waist level. A driver steered the truck around a half-mile track at about 20 m.p.h. and the student gunner tried to break targets lofted from hidden launchers along the way. On our first circuits most of us could claim only one or two hits out of 20 shots.

We soon learned a minor key for this thunderous tune. From the first week we had protected our ears with wads of cotton. Here, the secret to success came in removing the cotton so we could hear the twang of the launcher, even over the sound of the truck engine. We discovered that we could hit most of the disks if we knew when they took off. We didn't worry about any hidden price in damaged eardrums. The skin at our waists turned black and blue by the end of the week from flailing against the steel ring in the truck. Our Winchesters, although barely a month old, had worn so much that their pump mechanisms collapsed whenever we dropped the butts to the floor.

On Jan. 11 our strategic air forces lost 60 heavy bombers attacking German aircraft plants. But an offensive by the Soviet army that month broke through the German circle around Leningrad. In places Red armies had re-entered Poland. On Jan. 22 American and British forces landed on Anzio beaches south of Rome. At the end of the month an American invasion force landed in the Marshall Islands. The Allies clearly had started moving forward.

We began our fourth week with a trip to a ground-to-ground range which was being abandoned soon after construction. Those with air experience knew that shooting at ground targets from the ground would waste our time, but none of us could forget hearing for the first time a 50 cal. machine gun being fired close by. As about ten of us stood around a single mounted gun an instructor reached over and touched off one round. We all jumped as if it had been a seventy-five.

We thought our fourth week might kill us all. Some prodigy in Training Command planning thought we ought to shoot at ground targets--from B17s. The idea of getting to fly in Seventeens excited us all, but even in our inexperience we knew they had not been designed for low-level attack on ground targets. Nobody would use this plane that way against any enemy smarter than a canvas dummy.

Radio operators in combat would never fire from the nose, from ball turrets or from tail guns, so they put us in the top turret, at the radio gun and at the two waist guns. Students in other classes involving only gunners got to fire the 50s from every position.

We couldn't fire at ground targets from the top turret or radio room gun, so that left us manning the guns in the waist as the pilot flew us past canvas mock-ups of planes on the ground. We made most passes under 200 feet, and at that height air thermals rising from the desert hit us like waves of water.

Instead of our swinging the heavy machine gun, aiming and holding it on a target as we passed at 200 m.p.h., the gun swung the gunner, whose flailing feet rarely contacted the waist floor. After the first pass in which we shot at everything but the ground, we all refused to fire unless we could brace ourselves. Each of us had been given 200 rounds to fire on that first day and we brought most of our belts back to base.

There we soon learned that a lieutenant in charge of the training segment had gone in full cry for our skins, demanding to know why we hadn't used up our ammo. Two of us tried to point out to him the dangers of hitting the plane's wing or horizontal stabilizer, especially when as passengers, we'd go down with the plane. At that altitude we'd stand no chance of bailing out. The officer not only didn't listen but ordered us back to the same shooting exercise the next day.

Disgusted and afraid for our lives we spent most of that night searching for a safe solution. We decided finally to approach the pilot, whose tail we endangered as much as our own. Next morning we explained our problem to the pilot who had been assigned to us. His appreciation restored our conficence. He suggested that one of us might stand and fire the gun while two others anchored him in position, silly as that would be under real conditions. If that didn't work, he said, he'd let us fire our ammo harmlessly in the air on the way back to base.

We survived the week, drilling expensive holes in the sand and air, never once denting our plane. The training officer didn't tumble, and we discovered that no pilot on the base would talk to him. Nobody hit the dummy planes, so people in charge soon cancelled that phase of instruction at the school. We all learned again that if one doesn't look out for his own neck he can't always count on others to do it.

And so we progressed to air-to-air gunnery, spending half a day in classrooms learning the theory and the other half day applying it. We learned how all the turrets worked as well as their automatic gunsights. We studied and applied angle-off sighting for our hand-swung guns, lessons others had learned in the past year over Europe. We identified German and Japanese fighters from their silhouettes. We spent whole days in mock-up gun positions, firing beams of light at planes on movie screens.

In the air we fired at long cloth sleeves towed behind North American AT6s, reasonably fast advanced trainers. From top turrets, radio room guns and waist guns we fired rounds whose tips had been dipped in colored wax. Six of us rode in each B17, taking turns firing from the four positions, and each using ammunition bearing a different color. When all six had fired our rounds we'd return to base, find the right towing sleeve and count the holes, if any, showing wax in our color.

Our scores ran reasonably high on days that we fired from the Bendix top turret, a steady mount with an automatic gunsight, probably the best gun position on a B17. From the post-mounted stations in the radio room and waist we rarely scored more than a dozen hits as the sleeves attacked us in pursuit curves. We killed two tow cables in one day, wiping out any record of our scores, and shattered one tow pilot's nerves by putting two rounds through the tail of his AT6. It relieved us all to learn that he couldn't detect wax of any color around the holes.

Our shooting adventures turned up an incidental threat to our well being. In the top turret, at the radio room and at the waist positions, spent casings dropped to the floor. When a fresh gunner took over for a turn at a firing position, by habit he normally charged a new round into the chamber. Trouble was, the chamber already held a round which lay with its primer against a very hot bolt. Charging this "hot round" out of the gun caused it to drop to the floor where the impact often set it off. Several gunners reported to the dispensary with bits of brass embedded in their shins, and an order went around for us to avoid unnecessary charging of guns.

For a B17, Bendix made the top turret, behind the cockpit, and the chin turret, under the bombardier. Sperry made the ball turret, just behind the radio room. A combination of electricity and hydraulics powered servo units which moved these turrets and the two guns in each of them in response to the gunner's hand actions. The gunner stood in the open-sided top turret, making it easy to get in and out.

Automatic gunsights allowed the gunner to follow an attacking fighter, which he kept framed in reticles of red light, projected onto the sighting glass. As the gunner moved the turret and gradually changed the reticles to match the size of the plane in the sight his actions fed information to the sight mechanism regarding the plane's speed and distance. Guns often pointed at a different angle than the sight, which meant that the sight had compensated for the attacking plane's velocity and its distance. In the hands of a practiced gunner these marvels achieved an astounding kill rate.

On the ground we tried the Martin-made top turret which B24s carried. We found its action a bit jerky and its fold-up seat ungainly. In both B17s and B24s the ball turret, barely four feet in diameter, required a small gunner. I couldn't force my knees past the gunsight and never envied any ball gunner's job in cold, cramped solitude.

Experience in the angry skies over Europe brought one change we appreciated in aerial gunnery instruction. Until late in 1943 air-to-air gunnery students had stood in the rear cockpit of one AT6, firing at a sleeve towed by another. Bomber crews needed turret training, not the cold and wind of an open cockpit.

We heard one story about those earlier gunnery school days so often it must have been true. The machine gun on its mount in the rear of an AT6 carried a canvas chute to catch empty brass cartridge cases when they were ejected through its bottom. After some firing the chute sometimes jammed with spent rounds and required a couple of good whacks by the gunner to free it.

Most newly-arrived trainees had to be told this by the pilot, who communicated with the gunner through an ancient and noisy device called a Gosport tube. On this occasion the pilot noticed a pause in the gun's hammering and, figuring that the chute had become jammed, yelled into the tube:

"Hit the chute and save your brass!"

The gunner bailed out.

A B17 fuselage provided considerably more comfort and safety, in our opinion. We worked hard during that week of air-to-air gunnery, though, carting our 200 rounds of 50 cal. ammo through tight quarters, loading and un-loading guns, cleaning guns and gathering spent brass from the floor.

At Yuma we flew in F-model B17s in which the firing hatches or windows had to be removed at waist and radio room gun positions before we could swing the gun mounts into position for firing. With these windows out we noticed the wind and cold but still had no idea how bad it could get. In G-models, just then arriving in combat units, fixed windows each held a gun in a spring-loaded mount, providing both protection from the elements and help in moving the weapon. We wore newly issued but obsolete fleece flying suits, but never flew at truly cold altitudes.

Sometime in February my brother John won a three-day pass and arrived by train for a weekend visit. He had been taking classes as part of an ASTP Star unit on the UCLA campus. Because Yuma offered few charms we spent about a day and a half exploring the base and its planes. I got him a bunk in my barracks and during his short stay the Army Air Forces fed him as one of its own.

Because we all considered Yuma a poor place to visit, some trainees rode buses regularly to Mexicali, about 40 miles west and just across the Mexican border. Although livelier, Mexicali to me had all the appeal of a run-down am-usement park.

Over Germany at about this time P51s started escor-ting heavy bomber groups to targets. This marked the be-ginning of the end for devastating fighter attacks on our daylight formations.

For our last week of instruction we put 8 mm movie cameras on each gun or turret. Every day each of us picked up a film cartridge and put it in one of the cameras.

Changing gun positions from day to day, we "fired" at AT6s whose pilots made standard pursuit passes at us from every angle. Gunnery instructors then graded our shooting from the developed film and showed us how we had scored hits or made fatal errors. Although we did well only from the top turret, the week's effort convinced us that the best gunnery instruction lay in those little reels of film.

We graduated at Yuma with an extra Tech Order number in our folders along with the word "gunner." Assignment to a crew usually came next, we knew, so we expected orders to an assignment center. Instead, at the end of February we all received two-week furloughs. We boarded regular passenger trains on the first of March, thinking that this probably would be our last visit home before going overseas.

Author, right with Pfcs. Hefner and Phlamm
at Sioux Falls, S.D. radio school.

7. Coming Together

A first class ticket on a regular passenger train allowed me to stand in the aisles or sit on the end of my B-4 bag for most of that 2 1/2-day trip home to North Dakota. The promise of home eased any inconveniences. Civilians and servicemen filled even the washrooms. Most available seats went to women passengers, many of whom had gone to visit husbands or sweethearts in training camps.

Stops in stations along the way turned into frantic scrambling, even through the windows, to hunt for food and drink. After the first few stops we learned to stuff our small musette bags with sandwiches, candy and cold drinks. Who knew how long we'd have to wait for the next stop, and anyway, extra food always helped in making friends among the civilians.

After more than nine months away, even Ludden, North Dakota, a town of 150 people, looked pretty good. Eating your mother's food and visiting with old friends has a way of straightening one's view of the world. It didn't hurt that I could show off new corporal's stripes and a shearling flying jacket. People listened when one spoke, a phenomenon not enjoyed in all those months.

For people in this hometown as in others the war had grown in seriousness since casualty lists became a regular feature. A window in nearly every house bore its blue stars, and a few displayed gold ones. They represented faces with whom I had learned math and played baseball only months before. Residents knew new words like Bougainville, Kwajalein, Anzio and Cassino.

My parents asked questions all parents have asked since sons first went off to war: Where would the Army send me next? When did I expect to go overseas? When would the war end? Only the first had an answer. Furlough orders included instructions to report to the 2nd Air Force combat pool in Salt Lake City on March 17 for crew assignment.

Dad boarded the train with me on the 15th. We would ride together to Ogden, Utah. There he'd switch to a train going to Sacramento for a visit with John and enjoy a little vacation. The first day on the train we ate cold fried chicken my mom had packed, and on the second we ate pheasant sandwiches handed to us by folks at the North Platte, Neb., station. Altogether, we enjoyed the chance to visit.

Everybody in the world seemed to have piled into the base at Salt Lake City. Each air crew member, for hundreds of crews, having completed training peculiar to his duties, had been directed here to find that fateful union with nine others. Each of us displayed his own kind of confidence, if not a swagger, while hiding his apprehensions, if possible. We all knew deep in our souls that if the others knew their jobs as well as we did, we might be in trouble.

It took three weeks for assignment, weeks we spent anxiously trying to keep up with the war and to entertain ourselves. One zealous non-com, appearing out of nowhere one morning, hauled our entire barracks out onto a frozen field for PT. He suffered from one angry catcall after another for two hours and we never saw him again.

Someone set up a code practice room in a tent and several of us radio operators spent our afternoons there, trying to maintain our speed. We went into town at least twice a week, once to see a superb show by Blackstone the Magician.

The Royal Air Force lost nearly 100 bombers out of 800 in a March 30 night attack on Nuremburg. On April 5 the 15th Air Force began its oil offensive with an attack on Ploesti, Romania.

Assignment to crews came finally around the 10th of April for 560 officers and non-coms. We had orders to meet the others in our crews at specified places around the station. My fellow crew members, with whom I was to spend the next nine months, gathered in a corner of a post theater. As we drew together I heard a distinct cheer from one of them who had just been assured by our pilot that we would fly in B17s and not B24s. He and the co-pilot had trained in Seventeens, he said, as we shook hands and started trading names.

No more important decision came down in my behalf in all the war. During gunnery school we had learned that we'd probably go into heavy bombers, but we had no idea which ones. Because of our natural concern for our skins, even back in radio school we had debated the merits of bombers. Our interest turned especially to those qualities having a hand in getting their crews home safely. For us in this crew, Boeing B17s stood above B24s even before we flew in them as a team.

This was the crew that introduced itself that day:

Pilot: 2nd Lt. Philip Skok, Valley, Wash.
Co-Pilot: 2nd Lt. Dick Mabie, California.
Navigator: Flt. Officer Gerald Milburn, Kentucky.

Bombardier:2nd Lt. Charlie Grayson.
Aerial Engineer: Sgt. Dale V. Dolton, Chicago, Ill.
Radio Operator: Cpl. Jack Botts, Ludden, N.D.
Ball Gunner: Pfc. Ray Dickson, Tennessee.
Waist Gunner: Pfc. Albert O. Hall.
Waist Gunner: Pfc. Colin Davis.
Tail Gunner: Pfc. Edward Flood, Providence, R.I.

Within days we developed some lasting friendships. We could detect in addition a growing confidence, personally and collectively. Until now none of us had trained with or even associated with officers and men who would fly with us. Ties of trust and faith that bind military people forever to their units now made sense. To all of us so loosely involved for months in training commands the grand plan had begun to pay off. We had come together.

On April 11 all 56 crews boarded a train for Rapid City, S.D., for ten weeks of operational crew training in B17s.

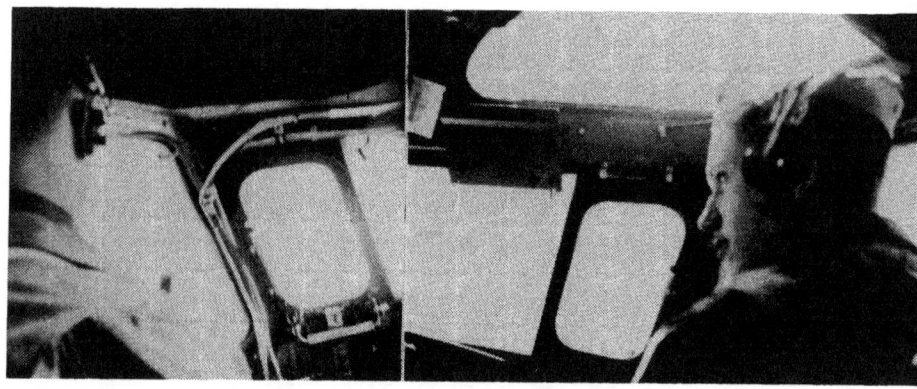

Pilot Phil Skok and Co-pilot Dick Mabie during flight.

8. Operational Training

The brass in command at Rapid City Army Air Base started the final training of a new collection of crews like ours every 10 or 12 weeks. People who had served at least one tour of duty in a combat bomber group now auditioned us to see if we had learned our lines for one of the most important roles of our lives. We spent at least four hours a day in special classes and on most days at least another four hours in the air as a crew.

In groups of eight or ten we sat in pressure chambers for several hours in simulated altitudes up to 35,000 feet. We had to learn how to use masks and regulators and the dangers of going without oxygen, even for a few minutes. Oxygen in a B17 came from four independent systems which supplied 16 separate outlets and regulators. Eighteen aluminum bottles, each about a foot in diameter and 18 inches long, held the supply and were stored behind the pilots above and below the flight deck.

An Army dentist drilled the silver fillings from my teeth and then refilled the holes. The pain, he tried to assure me, couldn't compare to that caused by a tiny, unfilled air space in even one tooth at the low pressures of high altitude.

Instructors checked Skok and Mabie for proficiency in flying at all altitudes, in and out of formation. At the same time other instructors took Milburn and Grayson over the

45

jumps in getting to a target and then hitting it. One old hand tested my code speed and the length of time I needed to change frequencies on the liaison radio. Dolton was checked on his knowledge of Wright Cyclone engines, and our four gunners peppered more flying sleeves.

Low altitude flying had made me a bit airsick in gunnery school. Now the malady struck again as we hit the practice ranges of South Dakota. After cleaning up my first mess in the bomb bay I made a lined barf box to use if necessary and carry away from the plane, leaving no evidence of my distress. This inner churning and nausea disappeared if I stayed busy at the radio desk. Anyway, when we climbed above those bumpy thermals all symptoms vanished.

Warmer temperatures of May and June added to our nausea, especially just before and after takeoff. A blistering sun made the aluminum skin of any plane too hot to touch. Without insulation, the fuselage of a bomber became an oven, evil-smelling too because of an anti-corrosive coating applied to everything at the factory.

Instead of climbing into our assigned plane to await taxi instructions, we sat in the shade of a wing until the last minute, Skok listening to the tower by way of a long phone lead. Once inside, we tried not to breathe, nearly expiring before cooler air started moving through the ship. Drenched in sweat, we then had to move fast to get into our cold temperature gear as the plane gained altitude. We soon became adept at timing this quick change, but such extremes from heat to cold left one's skin clammy and uncomfortable.

None of us could stay in the crew if airsickness persisted, and we lost Ray Dickson and Colin Davis in the first week. Both tossed their cookies every time they flew, so the flight surgeon grounded them despite their pleas for another chance. Within a day or two we had another ball gunner and waist gunner, two who stayed with us all the way.

Pfc. Theodore U. Kleiber, the ball gunner, came from Evansville, Ind., and we called him "Tuk" because of his initials. As long as we watched out for him, even to see that he changed his socks, he did well at his guns and as part of the crew. Pfc. Russ Grove, waist gunner, came from Toledo, Ohio, and performed well despite a short temper.

We flew at all hours for our gunnery, bombing, navigational, altitude and formation sequences. Each member of our crew, while being tested in his own duties, quietly and a bit anxiously watched the performance and behavior of the others. All four of our officers pleased and amused us, mixing ideal proportions of humor and seriousness, and demonstrating that they knew the difference.

Phil Skok flew a plane smoothly and effortlessly, and because a first pilot also commands the crew, he showed us he had talents beyond controlling a plane. An ideal crew boss, Skok flew and led with a coolness rare for one in his early 20s. A word or two from him put us in order under the worst circumstances because he knew when to reassure us and when to laugh at us and himself. We soon sensed that Phil could get a plane back to base if anyone could.

Co-pilot Dick Mabie, a tall, rawboned, red-haired Californian, joked his way through every trying, uncomfortable moment, playing a light-hearted second violin to Skok, the concertmaster. If the next hour's duty wasn't fun, he'd try to find a way at least to make it memorable. Except for takeoffs and landings, duties rarely handed to co-pilots, he handled controls as well as Skok.

Jerry Milburn, the navigator, and Charlie Grayson, bombardier, as unlike as two people can get, still pulled together like a matched team in the ship's nose. Milburn, small and serious despite his twinkling humor, had to balance Grayson's endless clowning and story telling. Each knew his job, and Grayson had even instructed at a bombardier's school for a time. We called this unlikely pair "Big Sol" and "Little Sol."

Sgt. Dale Dolton, the flight engineer, nearly always displayed a wide smile, and he understood a B17's engines, controls and instruments as well as his top turret. He normally stood behind the pilots, and on takeoffs and landings his eyes flicked from one instrument to another as he called out the air speed.

Dolton's special interest concerning the four engines had to be cylinder-head temperatures, RPMs and manifold pressures, 12 readings which had to stay within a narrow range. Off duty he knew how to have a good time, and rarely failed at it. He and I, the two technically trained non-com crewmen, soon joined up in missions to Rapid City. Ed Flood, tail gunner, a tall, dark-haired Irishman, often collaborated with us in exploring the attractions of this Black Hills town.

The military never quite forced Rapid City out of its quiet, bemused pace. Soldiers didn't overwhelm this place as we had Sioux Falls because we numbered in the hundreds here instead of thousands. We could get passes whenever evening or night flying didn't interfere, and on some weekends we had three-day tickets.

On May 18, when we had completed about half of our operational training, Cassino, the mountain roadblock in Italy, fell to Allied troops.

We spent one morning at the Rapid City base, as we had at gunnery school, learning the function and importance of our parachutes. Nobody looked out the window when this subject came up. Taking the advice of former air crewmen who had bailed out, we tightened our harnesses to where we could hardly stand. Each man checked out a little chest-style chute before every flight and stowed it near his crew position where, in a case of emergency, it would be available to snap easily onto the harness.

Every crew took its turn practicing bail-out and ditching. In a parked plane we jumped from our assigned bail-out positions onto mattresses on the ground. I left the plane through open bomb bay doors along with the pilots and engineer. Someone timed our actions from when the pilot sounded the buzzer until all of us had cleared the plane. We repeated our scurrying and hopping until we could clear out in less than eight seconds.

We never made real practice jumps, probably because those in charge knew we'd find the D-ring, somehow, and yank it in an emergency. Fully conscious crewmen rarely forgot that part if they had to leave the plane. A 15-foot static line, attached in the bomb bay, could be snapped to the D-ring of a wounded crewman's chute pack before he was rolled out of the plane.

We learned not to worry much about counting to ten before opening the canopy. At high altitudes and in flak areas it was better to jump and wait, slowing up and falling several thousand feet before pulling the cord. Opening the parachute soon after bailing out could wrench one's bones because of the higher speed. Also, one could pass out from lack of oxygen at high altitudes. Over a target, especially, a parachuter wanted to drop out of the flak before opening the canopy.

We practiced ditching a Seventeen from a mock-up plane that was moored on a pylon in the middle of Canyon

49

Lake, near town. The middle section of a wrecked ship, including radio room, had been rigged for our pleasure. A motor boat took us to this strange structure and we crawled in the top hatch of the radio room. Ditching procedure required seven crewmen to take stations there before a stricken plane landed in water. The radio operator's duties required him to send an emergency position report while still in the air, then he had to gather together all the survival gear, including a small radio.

In leaving a Seventeen after ditching, once forward motion had stopped, the two pilots and engineer had to crawl out the windows in the top of the cockpit and slide down to the wing. The radio operator's duty included yanking out the top hatch, stowing it and pulling handles that released two five-man dinghys, one onto each wing. While the rubber rafts inflated, the seven of us in the radio room pulled ourselves up and out of the open hatch and slid down the sides of the fuselage to the wings.

Then, five of us on each wing, we had to load two emergency packages into each dinghy, scramble in ourselves and shove away from the supposedly sinking plane. Our examiners wanted all this to happen in three minutes, but nobody ever claimed that record.

We put our trust in the B17, which floated like a duck if it wasn't smashed up. A fashionable story alleged that one ditched Seventeen had to be sunk by naval gunfire in the North Sea because it presented a menace to navigation. B24s on the other hand habitually drowned their crews.

We all wore "Mae West" life vests under our parachute harnesses, so we never risked drowning in the lake, but we grew to hate this exercise, whatever the urgency, because we never escaped a soaking in the frigid lake water.

The main "target" for our practice bombing had been laid out in the big bend of the Missouri River not far from Pierre in the middle of South Dakota. Little blue practice bombs with white marking powder plastered the circle without fail when Grayson aimed them. We in the crew agreed that he didn't need the practice, so after the first few days the rest of us took turns aligning markers in the Norden sight. Only Grayson's results deserved any admiration and our fumbling efforts made us appreciate his work.

Jerry Milburn checked me out on the radio compass one day while we cruised serenely over the South Dakota Badlands. As we sat at his desk in the nose he told me to find our position. He gave me a start signal and I tuned the compass radio to three commercial stations in the area. Then, scribbling down their bearings from us, I plotted those lines from each station, producing a tiny triangle on the map--our position. Milburn asked if I could come that close every time. I bet him a cigar that under those conditions my triangle would measure less than the size of a dime eight times out of ten. After several more practice plots he gave me his blessing and said he had better not break the rules by "gambling with the enlisted men."

Nobody lugged more gear than a navigator, and Milburn exhibited a most memorable study on his way from daily briefing to our assigned airplane. His high altitude clothing, parachute, oxygen mask, two briefcases of maps and his boxed chronometer and sextant made him an ungainly mound, propelled by a pair of flopping flying boots. Nine artless fellow crewmen abused his buoyant good nature.

His duties required that he plot our courses to and from our objectives and every turning point in between. Given a little lead time, he'd draw the plot in the ready room. If our briefing came minutes before takeoff he'd pencil his course lines as we took off and circled for altitude. I don't recall a time that he didn't have a heading ready when Skok asked for it. We razzed him endlessly, however, whenever he failed to cage the flux-gate compass to protect it before landing or maneuvering.

A perfectionist, Milburn always tested one method of navigation with another, or even two other methods, then asked me to check our position by radio. The two of us consequently spent very little time enjoying the South Dakota scenery. We took some pride in this, complaining in mock disdain about the innate laziness of bombardiers and gunners who obviously came along for the ride.

Training kept me as busy as Milburn. Our base station tried to avoid problems caused by inexperience in earlier combat radiomen. It sent me a new weather report every hour, plus new course and target changes, of interest to pilots, navigator and bombardier. In return, the base station expected a position report from me every half hour.

Before every practice mission the radioman picked up a code flimsy and tuned his liaison receiver and transmitter to the day's frequency. Then he set both of the pilot's command sets to proper frequencies and checked operation of the radio compass. He also had to check the ammo supply for the radio room gun.

Both ground and air operators sent every transmission in five-character bomber code. Radio operators kept a standard radio log, recording not only every transmission and time but every change of equipment and frequency. The operator decoded the cryptography of every incoming message and read it over the ship's interphone to the pilot or navigator. Because this wasn't combat, we didn't change our codes every few hours, but training included test-firing the flare pistol from its ceiling lock in the cockpit, using the

color code of the moment. Operators also practiced sig-
naling other planes with the Aldis lamp, again using the
proper code words and color.

Our four gunners, once they checked out against
attacks by flying sleeves, usually slept. We didn't blame
them much, except when their nearly lifeless bodies blocked
our movement. Waist gunners especially seemed to find my
radio room more comfortable than their own stations, so I
ordered them out, and Skok warned them to stay clear. One
persisted, however, flopping in his favorite spot against the
fuselage skin between me and the transmitter.

One day he leaned against my big double-throw antenna switch, the connection that allowed me to choose between a fixed and trailing antenna. I knew that one touch of
the transmitter key could send him a stinging message, and
in a moment he was on the radio room floor, shouting ob-
scenities about the mysteries of radio. He rarely crossed my
threshhold again.

We enjoyed Rapid City's hospitality, largely because
of its people. Most bars still offered free eggs, cheese and
crackers with their beer, and several churches and clubs held
regular dances at which young women and soldiers could
meet. We soon developed a pattern of calling those we had
met and arranging to meet them somewhere before going on
to a dance. Few if any among us had cars, so our transportation requirements dictated part of the plan.

We hitch-hiked throughout those beautiful hills
whenever we could put together a couple of days, getting as
far north as Deadwood and south to Hot Springs. One day
Charlie Lasota, a fellow radio operator, and I got to see the
faces at Mt. Rushmore soon after the sculptor completed
them.

At Rapid City the military formality we had known in the Training Command eased off to a satisfying level, calculated probably to break us in to combat-area informality. Ground crews and service personnel accorded us a mild deference we found embarrassing after having been ignored so many months. Because we flew at odd hours we could enter the flight mess at any time and order what we wanted for breakfast, our favorite meal. Jeep and truck drivers offered us rides to planes parked at the far end of the apron.

But we didn't cross the ancient and honorable line separating officers and men in our crews. Though we might sweat together and razz each other while working, we always returned in other settings to an easy formality. I don't remember ever saluting any of our crew's officers, but we lived in separate quarters and spent our social hours in two worlds. This division never seemed to embarrass anyone or stir resentment, probably because we never questioned it.

Rome fell to American troops on June 4 and two days later a combined American, British and Canadian army landed on Normandy beaches in France. We grabbed eagerly at newspapers and Armed Services reports to keep up. We speculated on whether events in Europe might have passed us by.

Two hundred planes in the 15th Air Force on June 2 began shuttle bombing between Italian and Russian bases.

By this time we flew most of our missions in formation, "bombing" strategic targets in the Great Plains area by way of cameras that attached in some way to the bomb sights. We sat through briefings before takeoff and interrogations after landing, and in many ways these practice flights cranked our bodies and minds into a professional attitude toward flying under stress. We rarely flew much higher than 20,000 feet, however, so we didn't prepare ourselves much for the cold.

We flew four days in April, 19 days in May and eight days in June, in B17Fs and Gs, the flights lasting anywhere from an hour and a half to five hours. We flew 13 missions at night. Except for one navigational mission I couldn't see much reason for the night flying, but it allowed a lot of crews to get a maximum of use from a few planes. It also gave us some practice at taking off and landing in the dark.

We flew one triangular course at night that I'll never forget, from Rapid City to Kansas City to Denver and then back to Rapid City. We didn't bomb anything, so I presume our instruction came in night navigation. We took off in a thunderstorm and I immediately lost contact with the base operator. Lightning then hit the trailing wire antenna and burned the reel to a bubbly black mass. Using the fixed antenna, I tried getting the base again, throwing in the "Q" signal meaning "anyone answer." A ham operator came on strong and I asked him or her in the clear to monitor my coded messages and relay them to the call signal of the Rapid City base.

This apparently worked fine. We flew our mission, landed without incident and everybody hit the sack. Next morning the base operator's log showed that my messages, sent every half hour, had arrived in Rapid City, but after we had landed. A listing of ham operators indicated that my benefactor of the night before lived in northern California.

In the middle of June we all got three-day passes, along with a promise of help to anybody wanting to try to make it home. One of the few who had a chance, I immediately caught a train east to Huron, S.D., to connect with a branch line that passed through Ludden.

A large window sill at the station in Huron provided a bed for the first night. I boarded the northbound train in the morning and managed to spend about 24 hours at home before having to ride the same trains back to base. A few others had put together more risky combinations of military flights to visit their homes for a matter of hours. Some of these returned a tad late, but nobody disciplined them.

We all knew the Army would send us into a combat area soon and we wouldn't see our families or homes again for a while. That's why that awful train trip seemed so worthwhile. We still had no idea where I'd go for my corner of the war, but my parents and I talked for hours, talk we would have missed if not for that three-day pass.

On June 19 we flew one fairly long formation practice mission to Oklahoma City where we had to "bomb" the rail yards and also fight off two squadrons of P47s. The fighter pilots, flying from somewhere in Texas, had almost completed their training too. Both bombers and fighters carried cameras on their guns to see if we had absorbed any of our training.

Most of the fighter pilots must have lost their way. Nobody in the B17s reported more than a handful, and only two made even half-hearted runs at us. We made bets with our pilots that their fellow throttle jockeys had spent the afternoon drinking beer at their officers' club. Officially, our top brass tried to pass it all off as a stunning success. If anything, we learned that those in charge fear bad reports so much that their own accounts drip with honey.

During takeoff for one of these missions Dolton, trying to provide air speed readings to Skok, yelled, "We've got no speed! We've got no speed!" Skok got the plane off the ground anyway, and Dolton, checking through a nose window, found that a protective sock remained on the pitot tube, the air speed measuring device. He found a big screwdriver in a tool kit and jammed it through the skin in the nose. Stationed at the window, Milburn gave him directions as he maneuvered the screwdriver and nudged the sock off. His actions added zest to our day, but we left him to explain the punctured plane to the ground crew chief.

My liaison equipment failed entirely during our last training mission, so having noted that in my log, I bummed around the ship. It allowed me to sample all the positions that had no occupants, stepping gingerly over sleeping gunners. The bombardier and tail gunner clearly owned the best views, but obviously they could see more at times than they preferred. Neither spot could compare with my own snug, if cold, cabin.

The tail gunner knelt in a tunnel where the cold and discomfort was exceeded only by that in the ball turret. Though my window over the left wing measured only about 10 by 12 inches, it offered a grand view of all I wanted to see.

For warmth, only the pilots and engineer on the flight deck enjoyed any heat in addition to that provided by their flying suits. There a heater running off the number two engine made high altitudes more bearable. We all wore what shearling-lined suits and boots we could scrounge from supply, because all the new electric suits went to Europe. Even at these reasonably low altitudes my feet warned me of bad days to come.

As we flew, meanwhile, we read and listened to reports of progress by our troops as they tried to break out of tiny footholds on the Normandy beaches. Between my

57

position reports and weather updates the big receiver provided news broadcasts and became a war information center for the crew. I simply had them switch their interphone position controls to "liaison."

On June 28, the day after American VII Corps troops took the French port of Cherbourg, we got our orders to pack up for a short train trip to Kearney, Neb., one of several staging bases for bomber crews heading overseas. We still didn't know where we'd go from there.

Milburn, working at navigator's desk.

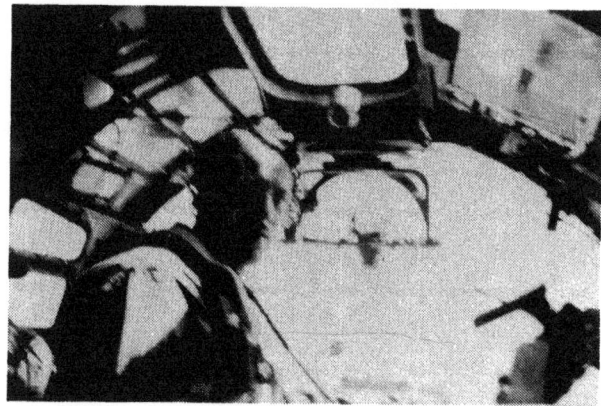

Grayson at his nose position.

9. Off to the War

Crewmen fresh from operational training at Rapid City saw a different kind of station as they got off the train at Kearney Army Air Base on June 30. Here the transient character of the crews, planes and schedules set the pattern. Bunks awaited us, already made up with clean sheets. We ate on schedule, but the cooks and their food made us feel like honored guests. We sensed a lot of changes in our status and couldn't escape making the analogy to lambs being fattened for slaughter.

Here personnel and logistics came together in obvious ways. The Army Air Forces arranged shotgun weddings of newly trained crews with new planes direct from factories. Both had to go overseas so why not send them together? Air Forces brass of all ranks swarmed over the base, presumably planning our future. The atmosphere reeked with speculation about the war and our places in it.

On the first of July Charlie Lasota and I paid a visit to Kearney. Since radio school this fellow trainee and I had often explored our surroundings together. This time we found a sleepy town of about 10,000 that seemed to tolerate visiting soldiers without making many demands of its own. It didn't provide bars, but we located a wine store and bought several bottles of passable stuff which we took with us to a central park.

There on a sunny bench we enjoyed our conversation, and the wine, all afternoon and far into the evening. The wine and warm air combined to put us to sleep. Stiff and a bit sheepish, we awoke some time after midnight. Returning to the base and to our sacks, we then slept almost until noon. Then the wine came back to remind us of its second-day effects. Our misery permitted no movement from our bunks despite shrill and derisive hoots from fellow crewmen.

The world and our bellies stabilized by the next day when all of us passed through a combat supply line to pick up new flying equipment and to replace worn uniforms. I kept my old OD's, but in outsize flight bags we carried away new parachutes and harnesses, heavy flying suits, boots, flying helmets, oxygen masks, light flying suits and leather jackets. In addition we each received a new .45 Colt automatic pistol in a leather shoulder holster.

That afternoon we rode a line cart to our new plane, the latest variation of B17G from the Douglas plant in Long Beach, Calif. The ship's log recorded 16 hours on its engines. Its freshness, even its smell, entranced us as we kicked its tires and examined every inch. We caught ourselves rubbing away our fingerprints with coverall sleeves. Early in 1944 the Army Air Forces had discontinued ordering planes sprayed in the dirty camouflage green and gray paint of earlier numbers. This one gleamed like a new cooking pot. A photographer from town snapped our picture as we stood beside it.

In France that day the U.S. First Army opened its battle of the hedgerows, trying to break through to the south.

We took our new ship for a 2 1/2-hour slow-time flight to calibrate the instruments and generally check it out. Every piece of radio equipment aboard performed well, and all of us, including Skok and Mabie, pronounced the plane ready to go, even to two extra fuel tanks, installed in the bomb bays. We decided that we'd take it. A more important question, however: where would this glossy wonder take us?

We learned some of that on July 4th, the very day we would leave. Summoned to a meeting, we filed with some apprehension into a darkened auditorium where a sheet hung over a map on the stage. A bird colonel started reading the names of pilots and handing them brown envelopes. Pilots on another list got another pile of envelopes.

The colonel said we'd all get details from our pilots, then he pulled the sheet away to show us our routes out of the United States. Though we had been given plenty of reason to believe we'd go to Europe, we produced an audible collective gasp when we saw that all the plots pointed eastward from Kearney. Nothing like facing the real thing. Most plots led to stop-offs in New England.

This officer asked if we had any questions. Someone whispered that it was sort of like asking condemned men if they had final requests. Then the colonel cautioned us not to tell anybody about our destination. I couldn't help but develop a mental image of Adolph Hitler--shrugging at the news of our coming to get him. The officer told us to send home all extra junk we wouldn't need. He wished us good luck.

Those in our crew circled around Skok, full of questions. He read a short note from the brown envelope and announced that after some stops on this side we'd fly from Newfoundland to the Azores in the Atlantic. Skok guessed that we'd fly to the Mediterranean area from there. More than half of the crews had orders to fly to Goose Bay, Labrador, meaning that they'd wind up in England. We returned to our barracks wondering again how the military could continue to dangle thousands of eager bodies on tentative strings.

It rained hard that afternoon but we briefed in the evening and got a weather clearance. Milburn and I got our navigational act together in the briefing room and then we all lugged our ton of junk to the plane. Somebody had stowed a bale of 20 new Army blankets in the plane's waist. We didn't need them as we sat in the steaming Nebraska evening waiting for taxiing instructions. Again, heavy thoughts of uncertainty overwhelmed our senses.

Takeoff came at about 11 p.m. Our first leap took us to Grenier Field, Manchester, N.H., where we parked at dawn with about a dozen other Seventeens from Kearney. After a night there we hopped up to Presque Isle, Maine, on the 6th. A day later we jumped to Gander Lake, Newfoundland, our springboard for the North Atlantic. Here crews from every branch of service appeared to wait for their clearance. This life as a transient crew appealed to us, meanwhile. The Air Transport Command met us with transportation, fed us well and even made up our beds.

During winter months a southern route often used in getting planes and crews to the Mediterranean area started in West Palm Beach, Fla. From there planes hopped to Trinidad, to Belem and Natal in Brazil, Dakar in Senegal and then to North Africa.

Just after midnight, the morning of the eighth, having piled on all the 100 octane aviation fuel we could carry, we lifted heavily off the runway and set a course in the darkness for Terciera Island in the Azores. Before takeoff a Red Cross van had delivered ten small box lunches to our plane, so we left chewing on cookies and apples. Because we had orders for radio silence I simply decoded half-hourly weather reports from Bluie West 1 and 2 stations in Greenland and the Crystal station in Iceland.

We flew at comfortably low altitudes so, unrestricted by oxygen hoses or heavy flying clothes, I roamed forward, delivering my weather updates by hand to Skok and Milburn. Skok and Mabie took turns sleeping in their seats and checking the autopilot and compass heading. Those two, and Milburn, Dolton and I stayed reasonably busy during the flight, mostly checking weather, engines and headings. Grayson and the four gunners slept wherever they could find a comfortable spot. The new Studebaker-built Cyclones never missed a beat at our deliberate cruising speed. Despite the many planes on that route we could have sworn we were alone all the way.

Just after dawn, expecting landfall, I went forward to the nose for a better view. Sure enough, directly ahead at Milburn's prescribed minute, we saw Mt. Pico and then Terciera. We landed at Lagens Field with enough fuel to have taken us to Africa, and parked with a group of our fellows from Kearney, eight hours and 40 minutes after takeoff. At this field, operational only a month or two, we felt a little surge of satisfaction in knowing that despite our youth we could perform flawlessly on demand.

U.S. Marines on that day mopped up the enemy on Saipan and our warships opened a bombardment of Guam.

Near the field we explored awesome windward cliffs pounded ceaselessly by angry Atlantic waves. Then we walked to an old Portuguese town where we bought about a dozen bottles of pink champagne. Never mind its lineage, or that questionable vintners probably had bottled it that morning. We hid these pink treasures away for future clebrations as if they had been laid down for the king of France. In the evening we sat through a movie on an open hillside near the field.

Next morning, the 10th, reloaded with fuel, we departed for Marrakech, Morocco, seven hours and 20 minutes away. This time we flew in bright sunlight, passing the Madeira Islands on our way. The base at Marrakech, obviously a part of the resupply chain stretching from combat areas to the States, impressed us as a magnificent sand box surrounded by cork trees.

Barefoot French Senegalese troops, about seven feet tall and wearing the red fez and red pantaloons, stood guard at a nearby stockade. The place was filled with German troops which the Allies had captured in Tunisia a year earlier. We looked for something cool to drink, having discovered a need for our canteens. Blazing sun and hundred-degree temperatures soon chased us into transient tents provided by the Air Transport Command.

Mess that evening turned into a struggle to overcome sand that permeated our mess kits and heat that stimulated waves of nausea. Water, milked from a Lister bag, tasted a mixture of iodine and the rubber that lined the bag. We theorized as we hit our cots that poor soldiers who drew duty here might survive a month or two before going mad and running off into the desert. In our cots after midnight we surprised ourselves by pulling wool blankets over us for warmth.

At this stage Skok picked up his orders from day to day, but clearly our arrow pointed toward the 15th Air Force in Italy. We said goodby to sunny Morocco on the 11th and flew along valleys of the Atlas Mountains on a six-hour jump to Tunis. We sailed over routes and passes bitterly contested by our armies in the early spring of 1943.

Though miles away from the airfield, Tunis, bombed and shelled heavily in that contest the year before, smelled to us like an overturned garbage can. In the evening we wandered through a graveyard of German and Italian planes, wrecked during bombings and bulldozed into heaps at the edge of the field. For a souvenir I wrenched a painted swastika from the tail of a Messerschmitt 109. Someone in the crew rescued a chronometer from another plane.

Next morning we hopped over to Gioia, near the instep of the Italian boot, passing over Pantelleria Island, Sicily and the Calabrian toe of the boot. Gioia obviously served as a resupply depot for crews and planes entering this arena. We learned here that we would deliver our plane to the 99th Bomb Group at Tortorella, about 100 miles north in the Foggia flatlands.

More important to us, we received orders to report to the 97th Bomb Group at Amendola, between Foggia and the Adriatic Sea. Next to being assigned to B17s, no other roll of armed forces dice could have had a greater and happier influence on our combat careers and ultimate wartime survival. We still hadn't learned the extent of our luck, but among service people and ground crews the word came through to us that the 97th was a "good outfit."

We flew to Tortorella on the 13th and handed our lovely lady over to ground crewmen who had been without a plane since flak had claimed theirs a few days earlier. We hated to leave that nice new ship but hauled our gear to a squadron mess where we ate lunch and waited for a truck from our new outfit. I sat for chow beside a flight engineer who told me that I'd like the "old 97th."

A six-by-six carried us about 20 miles over dusty roads and then turned off at an olive grove. We unloaded near a flat brick building surrounded by olive trees and faded six-man tents. Nobody paid much attention to us except for a first lieutenant who stepped out of the building. Cicadas nearly drowned out his words as he welcomed us to the 97th--and to the 414th Squadron.

Crew, standing from left: Albert Hall, Edward Flood, Jack Botts, Russ Grove, Dale Dolton and Tuk Kleiber. Kneeling from left: Phil Skok, Dick Mabie, Jerry Milbum and Chuck Grayson.

10. The Ninety Seventh

We had arrived as a replacement crew in the 97th Heavy Bombardment Group. As we made our first survey, nothing in our drab surroundings suggested the unit's distinction. In the days and months ahead, however, some details of its history and high regard seeped through to us from old timers in the ground crews.

The 97th had arrived in England more than two years before, the first U.S. heavy bomb group in Europe and the nucleus of the 8th Air Force. Eighteen of its air crews had flown the first U.S. heavy bomber mission in Europe in World War II. For that mission its commander, Col. Frank A. Armstrong Jr., led 12 B17Es from their base at Polebrook and Grafton Underwood on Aug. 17, 1942, to hit the Sotteville rail yards near Rouen, France. Six other Seventeens from the 97th flew a diversionary mission down the French coast.

Some of its pilots had never flown formation, some bombardiers had never dropped a bomb and some gunners had never fired a round. But despite its green crews the group persisted in the summer and fall of 1942, flying 14 missions against targets in northern France, learning its business every day. It was joined on Sept. 5 by the 301st group and on Sept. 6 by the 92nd. The first B24 group, the 93rd, flew in October.

Early in November the 97th and 301st received orders to support "Torch," the invasion of North Africa. In doing so they became the cadre of the newly formed 12th Air Force. Six planes from the 97th transported Gen. Eisenhower and his staff to Gibraltar on Nov. 5, and on Nov. 22 the group set up shop at Tafaraoui, a muddy airfield near Oran in Algeria.

From Tafaraoui the 97th flew the first 12th Air Force mission. It bombed targets in Tunisia, Sicily and Sardinia until mud at the Tafaraoui airstrip drove it on Dec. 24 to Biskra, across the mountains to the east. There a sandy field had been leveled in the Algerian desert much closer to targets in Tunisia. Later, in 1943, the group flew out of fields at Chateaudun in Algeria and Pont-du-Fahs and Depienne, both in Tunisia. After the Germans and Italians in Tunisia surrendered in May, 1943, targets switched to Sicily and Italy. The group became the first to bomb Germany from North Africa.

The 97th became the starting unit when the 15th Air Force formed in November, 1943, and moved to a field at Cerignola, Italy, in December. From there, near where Hannibal defeated two Roman legions during the Punic Wars, it flew the first mission carried out by the 15th Air Force. The group had been at Amendola, where we joined it, since Jan. 17, 1944. The group was part of the first shuttle bombing mission to bases in the Soviet Union on June 2.

The group was to receive a Distinguished Unit Citation for a mission Feb. 24, during what was called the Big Week, against the Steyr-Daimler-Puch aircraft components plant at Steyr, Austria. During that mission the 97th, leading the 301st and 2nd Bomb Groups over the target, obliterated the plant. When waves of fighters attacked the 2nd Bomb Group at the target, Col. Frank Allen, then commander of the 97th, released fighters assigned to him to go to aid the 2nd, leaving his own group unprotected. In the Big Week, starting Feb. 22, the 15th Air Force lost 93 bombers in four days.

We soon learned, however, that all of our good fortune didn't rise from the group's glories or accomplishments. Our advantages came more from being in the hands of ground crews, staffs and mission commanders with pride and good, solid experience. Although most flying crews had not been around more than eight months, all had learned their business from others who had taken lessons the hard way. Everybody knew what would work and what wouldn't, saving us much time and grief.

These folks, for example, not only had learned the tricks of formation flying and oxygen systems, they had organized and designed the present systems because of their early experience. Since the summer of 1942 they had discarded and rewritten the book on every procedure and piece of equipment. Of course they had passed their lessons on to other groups, but here we had the advantage of learning from the original pros.

We learned that when assigning places in missions the 15th Air Force handed the highest altitudes to the 97th. The brass at headquarters in Bari knew the group's ground crews could tune engines to reach those altitudes. The group often led in mass atacks on targets because it could be counted on to start the bomb run on time.

The 97th's ground crews and engineers had designed and installed slots in the outer wing sections of our B17s. These slots, soon added to all B17s, vented air from around the outboard or "Tokyo" fuel tanks and reduced the danger of explosions when flak punctured the cells.

Armorers from another group showed up one day for a lesson from our crews in how to change bomb loads quickly. Their group had missed a mission because an ordered bomb change had taken too long. Demonstrators from the 97th, instead of lowering each 500-pounder by cable to the steel mat below, released bombs from their carriers in the bomb bay with screwdrivers. Faces among our visitors turned an ash gray as each bomb hit the mat and was rolled aside. Within minutes the 12 bombs had been replaced by six 1,000-pounders.

George Gable, often our ground crew chief, and all the other chiefs, I'm certain, could diagnose problems in an engine simply by running it up while he watched the dials and listened. He knew from experience if a Cyclone needed changing or if he and his crew could keep it running. With help from the line mechanics they could change engines overnight if necessary to make the plane ready for a mission in the morning.

Our gunners didn't remove their guns after every mission, the practice in some other groups which slavishly followed the book. Gunners in the 97th cleaned their weapons at their stations. Ground armorers later checked them out and replenished the ammunition. For all of us who had one or more guns this saved an enormous amount of needless exertion and preserved alignment of the turret guns as well. Woe unto the hapless gunner, however, who tried to skip cleaning his barrels and bolts.

Every crewman in the 97th assigned to fly a mission attended the mission's briefing. We often heard complaints from crewmen in other groups that they had to fly to targets they knew nothing about.

We soon learned that nobody in our squadron or group cared a whit about our activities or location--except when Flight Operations had scheduled us. We could go wherever we wished and do what we wanted so long as we appeared for a mission or local flight as ordered. Few men could remember seeing a salute, even at group HQ.

We had joined an outfit close to our hearts, one we could believe in.

The "All American" from the 414th Squadron after a German ME109 sliced its fuselage with a wing over Tunis in 1943. The plane returned to base.

11. Tent City

Minutes after our arrival a 414th Squadron orderly took us in tow for a hot, dusty walk through rows of olive and almond trees. He left our four officers at a tent of their own and scattered the rest of us among tattered looking tents farther from the squadron headquarters building. We'd get our own shelter in a few days, he said.

Ed Flood and I moved in with part of another crew. For a cot, I claimed a stretcher lying near the entrance flap and dumped my gear nearby.

The four others in this tent belonged to the crew of a pilot named DeHaas. They had started their combat tour in England with the 8th Air Force. For some reason, perhaps a shortage of crews, the Army flew them to Italy and re-assigned them to the 97th. They seemed little concerned about having to swap Nissen huts in England for tents in Italy. Though heat and dust seemed to follow every step we made, the tent's sidewalls had been stretched horizontally, and we caught any breeze that passed.

Flood and I explored our surroundings that afternoon before chow and found that of the group's four squadrons only the 414th, 341st and the group HQ enjoyed the shelter of many trees under a hot Italian sun. Bivouac areas for the squadrons and group headquarters stretched along the north side of the asphalt highway. Ours lay easternmost, then came group HQ, the 341st, 340th and 342nd squadrons.

Our airfield had been made south of the road, building on a base originally constructed by the Germans. Three parallel runways, an asphalt and a steel mat strip, separated by a dirt crash strip, ran roughly northwest-southeast. A perimeter track of steel mat encircled the runways, giving off on either side every 150 feet or so to hardstands of more steel mat. Each hardstand held a resting B17. Greasy looking shacks at each stand provided temporary shelters for the ground crews. A gathering of line sheds and a makeshift control tower stood in the middle of the field near the runways. At some distance from the perimeter track we could see revetments for gasoline drums and bombs. A few wrecked and scavenged planes lay in a boneyard off to the southwest.

We learned that other bomber and fighter bases in Italy repeated this scene except for detail and size. Planes from the 2nd Bomb Group shared this field with the 97th, but the 2nd's men lived in a bivouac area two miles to the east on the road to the coast. Also, eight or ten Royal Air Force Halifaxes, a squadron attached to the RAF's 205 Group, sometimes flew from our base. They had skeleton ground crews and the planes usually clustered close together on mats at the south end of the field. The sound of revving engines, from planes taxiing, taking off or simply being tested, filled nearly every minute.

We walked over to group headquarters which occupied a tree-filled area a couple of hundred yards west of our own tents. A large state farm called Amendola once maintained offices here. The site consisted of several buildings surrounding a barn, about half of which was below ground level. The barn, probably 40 by 100 feet in size, provided reasonable space for briefings before missions--and for our movies. A wide, concrete animal ramp at the south entrance gave crewmen easy access. Flood and I found the communications office in a shack at the eastern side of the barn and we talked briefly to a sergeant.

After returning to our tent I dug out a V-Mail form and wrote a note home about my arrival:

> *July 13*
> *Somewhere in Italy*
>
> *Well, we've finally stopped traveling. It was a big trip, and we sure hated to give up the old buggy.*
> *Am sitting outside our tent on a pile of straw in the middle of what I think is an olive grove-- writing this on the back of my mess kit. Sure nice weather here so far, no fog anyway. . . I think I'm going to like it here OK. Just had a makeshift shower, and am going to have a K-Ration snack in a few minutes. All the comforts of home. Will have something to talk about when I am 60 years old. All for now.*

Squadron supply had offered us that pile of straw as filling for mattress covers. Doused liberally with lice powder the combination provided a bearable pad between hip and cot. My letter referred to fog in a lame and, as it turned out, fruitless effort to clue my parents to my location near Foggia. It seemed that since North Dakota has little fog they'd tumble to my clue. The plot failed despite my having coached them rigorously during my last visit. Although we had been thrust suddenly into pretty primitive conditions, my letter tried to paint a reasonable scene.

Meanwhile, Dolton and the three other gunners had learned that the squadron would check Dolton and me again for proficiency at our jobs. In a day or so we'd start taking local check flights with some old-timers, meaning people who had been around at least a month or two.

Next morning a six-by-six took all of us and our store of new flying gear to a line shack where somebody assigned each of us a wooden bin. It was to hold our zippered bag full of flying clothes, Mae West, oxygen mask, parachute harness and pack. Into the bag, in addition, went a 20-pound flak vest, flak helmet and newly issued electrically-heated suit.

Because of their cold crew positions, Flood and Tuck got the newest satin-finish green suits which included heated gloves and shoes. The rest of us got "blue bunny" suits, F-1 models that looked like electric blankets that had been re-sewn into bulky coveralls. The prospect of outside heat overjoyed us in any case. As radio operator I drew a new hack watch, one of the few perquisites shared with the officers in our crew. We kept our .45s with us.

We learned that after briefing for our bombing missions we'd ride trucks to this crew shack, pick up our flight bags, then ride to our assigned plane. Some of our questions had been answered.

Folks at the line shack confiscated an intriguing part of our parachute harness, issued back in Kearney. A flat felt pad about two inches thick made a kind of seat for the harness. Shaped openings in the felt held equipment to help us escape in case we had to bail out in enemy territory.

The escape kits seemed to have been designed for New Guinea rather than Europe. A folding machette, maps, bars of concentrated food, flares, medical kit, fishing hooks and line, matches, money and compass had occupied our interest for hours. Reluctantly, we turned these pads over to a sergeant, but only after taking out what we wanted. We had learned that in the Army, forced confiscation of any object usually means somebody else will enjoy it rather than you.

From the line shack we went to the big briefing room (barn) at group where an intelligence officer lectured us on the state of the war. He gave us some history of the group, the kinds of targets we'd attack and procedures in case the Jerries shot us down. His practical advice if we landed on enemy soil: Jerry knew as much about our activities as we did, so we shouldn't worry about giving up military secrets.

During the lecture the 97th's planes came rumbling over the base, back from a mission to Budapest. As we left the big room, crewmen jumped off trucks in the yard outside. We watched with some awe as nearly 300 tired and dirty men accepted doughnuts and lemonade at a Red Cross van and headed for interrogation.

Those who wanted it slugged down a shot of rye whisky before telling intelligence people what they had witnessed. Several reported counting six parachutes from a burning plane in another group. Despite the intensity, their reports added up to a successful and relatively uneventful mission. Considerably sobered, however, we in my crew walked back to our squadron area with men who had added another number to their string of missions.

On my improvised cot before evening chow another letter home took shape:

Italy
June 14, 1944

Well, our second day here has not found any change to speak of. Got a short haircut because it is easier to take care of, and a sunburn because I left my shirt off. There should be some good swimming here--much like that at Clearwater. . .

So far the dust has been the only bad part here. . . The chow is very good. . .

Haven't started anything yet. It won't be long though. . .

Our tent mates had told us about the lido, a beach on the Adriatic at Manfredonia, about 15 miles to the east on our road. Heavy American and British military truck traffic provided good hitchhiking, so we resolved to try it.

Next morning, however, we started local test flights, along with two or three planes carrying other new crews. Experienced crewmen rode along, coaching us on our procedures. Our pilots learned how to join up in squadron formations with other planes soon after takeoff. They also learned how to fly in the closest formations I had seen.

The operator at our base, codenamed "New York," gave me a workout along with all the procedure regarding codes, weather reports and bomb-drop reports. Each squadron received a code name for each mission, like "Backstep." Its leader on any mission became, for example, "Backstep leader," and any individual plane, because of its position, became "Backstep Baker," or "Backstep Charlie."

We flew five of these practice flights in eight days, each lasting only two or three hours. After the first one the examiners excused our four gunners, who managed on most of these days to get to the beach. I also spent hours testing out in a squadron code tent where I mixed perspiration with my envy of the gunners.

Some information that went into letters during this time:

Italy
July 16, 1944

. . .Have just finished brushing my teeth, shaving and washing--all with one pint of water. . . We have a PX card for "extras" which we buy once a week when the PX (tent) opens. We get 4 bars of candy a week, 1 bar of soap every 2 weeks, 7 pkgs of cigarets a week if you smoke, one can of fruit juice every two weeks, one Coke a week, four cans of beer a week (I sold mine to Dolton after tasting it). . . We get our candles, T paper and mosquito repellant, etc. from supply. We can get our laundry done at a farmhouse down the road. . . Grove and I hitch-hiked to the beach and went swimming yesterday. Had a good time. . .

They had an Italian variety show for us last night. Pretty good. They had a 14-year-old Italian girl who sang American songs in English. . . Haven't done any work yet, but will soon, I think. After all, it is what we are here for. . .

Italy
July 18, 1944

. . .I wish you could have seen some of the crops I've seen so far. . .The flowers in the little towns over toward the beach are the most beautiful I've ever seen.

Italy
July 20, 1944

. . .Will get put to work soon and the sooner the better--may as well get going.
You probably read in the papers about what the outfit is doing. It's in on all of it too.

On that day in East Prussia, German army dissidents tried and failed to kill Adolph Hitler.

Italy
July 21, 1944

. . .Finished getting checked out today, so will get down to work soon, I hope. . .
Have been going to school an hour every afternoon, so don't get over to the beach as the rest of the guys do nearly every day. . .
Lasota is in the same group I am in, but in a different sqd'n.

Italy
July 22, 1944

I got up early this morning before it got hot and took a swell shower. If it wasn't for that shower, I don't know what we would do. . .
I haven't taken part in anything yet, but will soon. . .

All this time the officers, Dolton and I flew check rides up and down the Adriatic. We caught rides in trucks over to the beach as often as possible to fight the unrelenting heat and dust. Because the medics considered Italy a malaria area we took atabrine tablets every day and crawled under suspended mosquito nets to sleep.

On one of these days the DeHaas crew, less the bombardier and gunners, slid a new B17 into a hillside north of us in the Gargano spur that juts into the Adriatic. They had been flying a slow-time check of a newly-delivered "Mickey" ship, equipped for radar bombing. They had approached the coast too low and without using enough power to overcome downdrafts off the mountains.

The engineer, Paul Fridrich, who slept next to me, came back to camp two or three days later and reported their experience. They had taken out a whole swath of trees and wrecked the plane, but suffered only cuts and bruises. A British Army forestry group had picked them up, tended to their wounds and hauled them out of the hills. The top brass court-martialed Jack DeHaas, fined him $100 a month indefinitely and suspended him from flying one month for wrecking an expensive plane.

Our crew of non-coms got a tent of our own on the 24th, except for Hall and Dolton who continued to live with another crew. This shelter, though old, leaky and gray, boasted a frame door. Two old-timers from another crew would live with us as they completed their missions.

Part of a letter home that day:

Italy
July 24, 1944

Well, I've got a new home. We have a new tent now and have it all fixed up. . . Instead of a dirt floor, this one has big slabs of rock on it. We even

*have a lantern. There is a sort of rack affair in the
center to hang our stuff on too. . . There is nothing
going on today so I think we will all go down to the
beach and go swimming. Maybe we can find a sail-
boat. . .*

*Milburn and Grayson aren't with us any-
more. They paid a visit to the "Fatherland" the
other day and took a notion to stay there. They are
all right. Sure miss them. . .*

Not all right by any means, Milburn and Grayson
had become casualties before the rest of us got to fly in
combat. The squadron was short of navigators and bombardiers, so it pressed them into combat assignments ahead of
the rest of us. The group flew to Brux, Czechoslovakia, on
the 21st and other crews reported Milburn's plane went
down smoking. On the 22nd the group went to Ploesti, Romania, and Grayson's plane was shot down over the target.

Such pieces of news in close succession nearly devastated us. We talked about it but could scarcely comprehend
the loss of two close friends who simply left our midst. I debated whether to mention it in my letter. The squadron
picked up their gear and listed them as missing in action.
We couldn't help but ponder our own first missions.

We did get to the beach that day, along with Skok
and Mabie, who were probably trying to divert our attention
from the bad news. We rented a fishing boat for a couple of
packs of cigarets and took it out into the Adriatic. About 30
feet long, the heavy wooden craft had a pointed sail
attached to a slanting boom that wore against a short mast.
None of us carried a compass and we scared ourselves when
we moved out of sight of land. We got our bearings from

the sun, finally, and after a lot of confusion sailed our craft back to Manfredonia.

The next day the U.S. First Army launched its breakout push near St. Lo, France, behind a concentration of 4,000 tons of bombs.

One of these days we took pictures of each other near the tent. Using my camera, the only one in the crew, we also photographed ourselves at the beach.

We had all been awaiting our first mission posting, and the big day came for most of us in the crew on July 26. After chow on the evening of the 25th we checked the flying assignment list on the bulletin board. The squadron operations officer had scheduled all of us for the next day, but had scattered us in other crews. The 97th had started this practice more than a year earlier and it had been adopted universally in the area.

Flying new crew members with old crews for four or five missions worked smoothly. New crews needed the experience and calming influence of the old timers. Old crews needed people to fill empty slots caused by casualties or by absence of those who had already completed their required missions.

A kind of somber excitement filled our tent that night. We didn't talk much about the next day, but I remember getting out some pencils, my long johns, wool socks and coveralls. Those things seemed more important than chatter about matters still not experienced. I did resolve that after every mission I'd write a short record of what happened.

12. Organization

When we arrived in July the 15th Air Force had been allocated all the bomber and fighter groups it would get, the latest of its B24 units having arrived in May. This air force, commanded by Maj. Gen. Nathan F. Twining, consisted of one wing of six B17 groups, including ours, 15 B24 groups, seven fighter groups and a few squadrons of photo and weather reconnaissance planes. The Seventeens and most fighters nested at fields in the Foggia plain, but some fighter groups based a ways north along the coast. The three wings of B24 groups flew from fields to the south of us, mostly west and south of Bari.

The 5th Wing, commanded by Brig. Gen. Charles W. Lawrence, had six groups: the 97th and 301st, which started in England in 1942; the 99th, which arrived in North Africa in March, 1943; the 2nd, which arrived in North Africa in April, 1943; the 463rd, which came to Italy in March, 1944, and the 483rd, which arrived in Italy in April, 1944. The 301st in 1944 flew from Lucera, northwest of us; the 99th was based at Tortorella, the 463rd at Celone and the 483rd at Sterparone.

A group headquarters performed a little like a World War II regimental headquarters in the infantry. It supplied the officers and non-coms for directing and co-ordinating operations of its squadrons. The 97th, commanded in July, 1944, by Col. Elmer J. Rogers Jr., received operational orders from 5th Wing headquarters in Foggia, which in turn received its orders from the 15th Air Force in Bari. Each group like ours usually flew its squadrons together in formation for a mission.

Group command in addition to the colonel included an adjutant and officers in charge of intelligence, operations and engineering. These ranked normally from light colonel down to captain and each had his own staff. The group maintained a small weather staff and a communications office with an officer and staff of non-coms who took care of our codes and communications with the base.

Group engineering had maintenance and repair staffs who operated from sheds out on the field. Several line officers each headed a separate division to organize and coordinate work by ground crews from the squadrons. Squadrons reported their problems and needs to these line chiefs who arranged for help with people, equipment and supplies.

Squadrons like the 414th corresponded somewhat to Army battalions. Lt. Col. Robert E. Stephens commanded the 414th while I was there. Each squadron also included an adjutant, an operations officer to organize and assign crews for missions, a flight surgeon and officers in charge of sections for intelligence, communications, engineering, ordnance, armament and supply, all captains or lieutenants, and all with staffs. A squadron had a complement of non-coms and orderlies for the paperwork, a supply sergeant and a mess sergeant, each having his usual slaves. A squadron's Table of Organization specified 443 enlisted men and 68 officers, but real numbers varied almost day to day as crewmen arrived and left.

Squadrons kept 10 to 14 planes under ideal conditions and 17 or 18 air crews like ours. Every squadron had an engineering section of two officers and about 100 enlisted men. A line chief in charge had three flight chiefs, 12 crew chiefs and 48 mechanics. A crew chief with four mechanics looked after one B17. Electrical, instrumental, sheet metal and propeller specialists could work on any B17 according to need.

If planes in one squadron suffered unusual battle damage, group designated mechanics from other squadrons, sometimes even planes, to fill in. Special crews refueled gas tanks, recharged oxygen bottles and loaded bombs. Ground crews like ours, most of whom had gone overseas in 1942, knew their business.

During my time in the group each squadron usually flew seven planes in a formation, or "box," so the group formation totalled 28 planes flying in four squadron boxes. This group formation, perfected since 1942, placed a maneuverable mass of planes over a target and a desirable pattern of bombs in the target area. It also offered a good overlapping of defensive gunnery against fighters.

A vee of three planes led a squadron, with another vee tucked in behind it, plus a seventh plane stuck in the rear slot. Planes within vees staggered their altitudes, that on the right wing high and that on the left wing low. The slot plane flew behind but lower than the vee leader. Each pilot and his crew took turns leading the squadron.

The four squadrons usually formed into a group diamond formation, one squadron in each of its angles. "Able" squadron, or box, led. Squadrons took turns in assignment to "Able Box." "Baker Box" on the right wing of the group flew a couple hundred feet higher than "Able," and "Charlie" on the left wing flew that much lower. "Dog box" in the rear flew lower but directly behind "Able."

This staggering of altitudes not only allowed the best coverage by gunners but reduced chances of one plane or squadron flying through the prop wash of another. Prop wash caused a lot of pitching and instability in a plane flying through it. Bad enough in ordinary formation flying, it could cause inaccurate bombing and even collisions between planes. Planning of formations never adequately solved the problem of crewmen falling into the props of planes behind when they had to bail out before their pilot could pull off to one side.

Groups sometimes flew in two attack units, each containing two or three boxes. The second attack unit flew a thousand feet behind and 500 feet higher. Any bomb group in the air force on the other hand might on rare occasions send only one squadron to attack a small target like a bridge or small rail marshalling yard.

The group commander, another top group officer or a squadron commander usually rode in the co-pilot's position in the lead plane in Able Box. On big missions in which several groups, even a wing or more, attacked a target in succession, the crew flying the lead plane in the lead group might play host to a couple of wing or air force generals. News that they had drawn lead position for a big mission would set off wild betting among the crew on how many stars might show up. Odds seemed to depend on how sexy the target--and how dangerous.

Until April, 1944, the 15th Air Force had four fighter groups to fly escort, three flying P38s and one equipped with P47s. Two groups transferred from the 12th Air Force that month, trading their Spitfires for P51s, and the group flying P47s also replaced their planes with P51s. A P47 group arriving in May had replaced its planes as well with 51s. That gave us three P38 groups and four of 51s to provide cover, good news for all bomber formations. In order of preference crewmen in our squadron usually listed P51s at the top, then P38s, P47s and Spitfires.

Orders for bombing missions took form sometimes days in advance at 15th Air Force offices in Bari. Brass there followed the policy and sometimes the special requests of theater commanders. These orders included target specifications, number of groups, fighter escorts, types of bombs, fuses and timing. When orders called for an attack by no more than one group per target, of course, the air force's groups fanned out to destinations in all directions.

Such orders usually arrived a day ahead at wing headquarters which decided which of the wing's groups would attack which targets. If the orders called for several groups to strike a single target in succession, time, heading and altitude for each clearly became critical. Orders usually specified a different heading and altitude for each group to throw off German defenses. No ground forces attacking enemy troops needed more planning to avoid confusion than we did on these "maximum effort" days.

Headquarters brass at groups which had been selected for missions received orders pertaining only to them. Group engineering people informed squadron engineering about how many planes had to be ready. The group operations officers, intelligence personnel and group bombardier and navigator plotted the attack route, prepared details of the AP, or aiming point, and collected information on enemy defenses. The weather officer pulled together the latest information he could supply for the briefing.

Orders dispatched to squadrons for the mission essentially involved the number of crews and planes, bomb loads and takeoff time. Ordnance people trucked in bombs and ammo. Gas trucks, loaded from a pipeline on the highway, filled tanks on planes scheduled to fly.

On the evening before a mission the squadron operations officer prepared a list of crews, including each individual crew member, and matched this list with serial numbers of planes in which the crews would fly. If the squadrons in any group couldn't expect to get the required number of planes ready, wing headquarters and even air force brass knew about it. In such cases the group normally would "stand down" for "maximum maintenance."

A stand-down gave air crews a day or two off, but it meant that ground crews worked day and night to repair damage. During July and August, 1944, nearly every group in the air force declared days for maximum maintenance because of damaged and lost planes. To make up losses, new planes and crews like ours seemed to arrive daily, along with truckloads of new engines and other parts.

Only the top brass at group and at squadrons knew the night before which target we'd go for the next day.

The author in the Adriatic at Manfredonia.

13. Beginnings

The plane ahead of us had started its takeoff roll when we turned from the perimeter track onto the runway. One of our engines coughed and the brakes screamed as the pilot blasted the tail around. We sat there for a moment, the Cyclones revving to takeoff power settings. About the time the plane ahead reached mid-runway, the pilot of our plane let his brakes go and we began our own accelerating run.

On takeoffs the pilot advanced the throttles but the co-pilot took them as soon as the engines hit maximum power at 2500 rpm. Cowl flaps were open for takeoff, props set at flat pitch for high rpm and turbos at 46 inches of manifold pressure.

Our little control tower and line shacks rushed past my little window. We rode hard at first, but as our speed increased the load shifted from wheels to wings, smoothing the bumps. Both wing tips moved up as they flexed to take the weight. In the middle, like a basket suspended on a horizontal string, swung three tons of bombs, 2,850 gallons of fuel, 13 guns and a crew of 10.

The sound of four straining engines bore into our senses through helmets and earphones. Finally, near the end of the runway at a speed of about 120 mph, all three wheels made one last tentative contact with earth. Freed, the ship crabbed a touch into the wind.

Scarcely had the wheels and flaps retracted when the pilot cranked the plane over into a tight, climbing left turn to catch the lead element of our squadron. We slipped into Dog position where we would lead the second vee. Engine rpms and turbo settings eased off to more sustainable levels, probably 2300 rpm and 38 inches, and cowl flaps were closed. The fuel mixture stayed at auto-rich as the squadron climbed at about 135 mph, indicated air speed. Time to pull heavy clothing and combat gear from our flight bags. My watch indicated a little after 6:30 a.m.

My first bombing mission had started before 4 a.m. that day, July 26th.

"Botts, Flood, Grove, Kleiber! Briefing in one hour!"

A squadron orderly had yelled through the door of our tent and moved on to the next. Already, rattling mess kits marked trails of air crews heading for the chow tent. In moments, after pulling on long johns, coveralls, wool socks and GI shoes, the four of us joined the rag-tag body of men stumbling through the darkness.

French toast, fried the night before in a batter of powdered eggs and powdered milk, awaited us in the chow line. Each man forked several cold slices out of GI cans into mess kits and drowned them in Karo syrup. The soggy bread filled our bellies and guaranteed a gas-free day at high altitude. Hot, black and sweet coffee topped it off, but only half a mess cup to discourage trips to the plane's relief tube. Old-timers already had filled our heads with stories of unfortunate crewmen who stuffed themselves with sausage, onions or cabbage before a mission. I never saw a technical manual on that subject.

Ground crews had been up a couple of hours, checking their planes and running up engines. Some, fighting balky machines or instruments, hadn't been to bed. Plenty of time for them to sleep after the group departed for its target. We could hear engines in the distance, rumbling and backfiring as we headed down a path toward the group briefing building.

As we filed into the room I found the pilot and crew to which I had been assigned and sat with them near the front. Skok, Mabie and the others, all like me, sat with crews we didn't know.

Attention among the 300 or so in the room had switched almost immediately to a large blackboard at the right side of the lighted stage. The crew's flight engineer, sitting next to me, whispered loudly:

"Weiner Neustadt, our goddam target. Here's the Old Man."

Col. Rogers, the "Old Man," walked out on the little raised stage, shading his eyes from a bright overhead light as he looked us over.

"Good morning, folks."

He stepped back to remove a sheet from a mounted map of central Europe, maybe 10 feet square. Black ribbon or tape stretched from our base in Italy in changing angles northward to a point just south of Vienna. Another tape formed still different angles in a path back to Amendola. The lines appeared to avoid circular spaces cross-hatched on the map. Those, according to the flight engineer, indicated known flak areas.

The colonel identified our target, an aircraft engine factory. He wished us luck and turned to a group operations officer who pulled down a white screen. An opaque projector heated up behind us and offered an aerial photo of flat buildings with saw-toothed roofs, squatting amid other buildings and railroad tracks. A white line drawn across the picture indicated our bomb-run course. A white cross on one building showed us the aiming point or AP.

He told us we could expect both flak and fighters at and near the target. He emphasized timing at the bomb run because the mission included the 301st and two other B17 groups. He'd fly the lead plane, he said, pleading with the pilots especially to maneuver carefully just after bombs-away so as to avoid collisions.

He retreated to the side of the room and a weather officer moved forward to give us bad news: He expected a mass of clouds to move into the Vienna area later in the day. He didn't sound optimistic that we'd even see the target, let alone bomb it. A P38 weather plane would fly over the area as we approached it and give our leader the latest word on clouds.

A group intelligence type presented his theories about the best escape route to take in case we had to bail out. Behind me I could hear cynical comments about our chances on the ground. The S2 officer gave us a time hack and waved us away.

Gunners moved outside to waiting trucks. Pilots met with the operations planner near the stage to work out the order in which they'd taxi. Navigators gathered with the group navigator to update their plots and bombardiers went to confer with the group bombardier. I and other radio operators hiked around the side of the building to the group radio office to pick up our logs and code flimsies. A sergeant there, handing me the little sheaf of rice paper, reminded me not to break silence, even in tuning up.

A six-by-six truck took about 20 of us to the squadron's crew shack on the field where we pulled our big flight bags from their bins. Outside, I found another truck that would take several of us to planes of the 414th. The driver pulled onto the circular track and soon started calling out the last three numbers of each plane's serial as he passed its hardstand. Hearing a loud "Yo!" in response, he would stop, allowing one or more heavily laden crewmen to jump off.

I got off at my assigned plane and struggled with the ungainly canvas container toward dim images in the darkness. The engineer I had sat with at briefing and the pilots stood talking with the ground crew chief. One engine apparently had caused some anxiety earlier but now had passed muster. I listened a moment, then awkwardly headed for the waist door.

The right cheek of this Seventeen labeled it the "Windy City." I guessed that someone in this or some other crew claimed Chicago as home. In the radio room I dropped my flying gear then dragged the frequency meter from under the desk and started tuning the big receiver and transmitter to the day's wavelength. The signals I produced didn't go to the antenna and couldn't be picked up more than a mile or so away.

During this procedure I discovered that instead of a standard bucket seat I'd have to sit on a wooden ammo box. The ball gunner, checking his equipment just beyond the bulkhead door opening, explained the lack of furniture. During a mission a few weeks earlier the pilot had shut down two damaged engines. To lighten the ship the crew had jettisoned guns, ammo and everything else that could be torn loose. The seat at least had gone for a good cause.

Next, I checked my flimsy and plugged four specified crystals into the pilots' VHF command set under the radio room's center floorboard. This gave pilots four air-to-air channels they could change by punching buttons on the upper control pedestal near the throttles.

After that I went forward to the cockpit and tuned in a weather station with the radio compass to make sure it worked. Passing through the bomb bay on the way back I counted twelve 500-pounders hanging serenely from their racks. Copper arming wires looped from release switches to propeller vanes on the bombs' nose and and tail fuses. In the radio room again a suck or two at my oxygen hose which hung beside the desk activated white lips on the regulator to assure me that we'd get along fine.

Outside in the cool morning air I joined other crewmen who now mostly stood or sat about on the steel mat, awaiting takeoff time. The first dim glow of dawn gave us a better look at our surroundings. Trucks had refueled all planes during the night, but now ground crewmen topped off our main tanks to replace fuel they had used in running up the engines. They jacked at wobble pumps to force 100 octane gasoline from 55-gallon barrels into the wings. One of the gunners filled his cigaret lighter with fuel that drained off the rear edge of a wing.

A Jeep rolled up and its driver tossed us a heavy paper bag. Somebody yelled at him as he drove away:

"I hope to hell you gave us some dinners this time!"

The crew divided the bag's contents and, not understanding the urgency, I wound up with what remained: a box of K-rations marked "Breakfast." Our lunch, obviously. The co-pilot explained that of the three K-ration meals most crewmen liked "dinners" best because of the little can of cheese. In "breakfasts" the cans contained a hard, salty mixture of cooked egg and bacon. "Suppers" provided hash, just as salty. These little brown, waxed boxes also offered us a fare of three dark, hard crackers, three cigarets, two pieces of hard candy or dextrose, some OD toilet paper and concentrated coffee or lemonade.

A shaft of green light from the tower sent us into the plane to start our engines. The pilots went through a pre-flight check list. Then the co-pilot primed, meshed and started Number 1 and the other engines in order, all back-firing and smoking in protest. My folded parka padded the ammo box. Unnecessary anyway, it might at least comfort and warm my backside. Several other planes taxied past us before the pilot gunned the outboard engines and took his position in the lineup. The smell of half-burned oil and fuel soon filled the plane. As we sat waiting our pilots tested magnetos and turbos at various power and propeller settings. Screaming brakes merged with engine sounds as the plane essed like a snake around the perimeter track, perhaps 50 feet behind the plane ahead.

Nervous attention probably described my condition as we approached the south end of the runway.

Dale Dolton, sitting beside his turret.

14. All for Nothing

The coveralls came off and the blue electric suit zipped over my long johns as we circled the base. We led the second vee in Baker Box and during our dressing act parts of Charlie and Dog boxes formed up. The coveralls went on again over the electric outfit. Then came zippered boots of rubber and sheepskin, something like a hunter's shoe-pacs but bigger, to fit over GI shoes.

The big .45 in its shoulder holster went over the coveralls. Next, the Mae West, a stiff, rubber and fabric life vest, slipped over one's head and then fastened with loops around the waist and under one's crotch. Pulling two cords at the bottom would puncture CO_2 canisters and inflate it if its user went into the water. First, however, the wearer would have to shuck the parachute harness.

The harness of thick, stiff cotton webbing snapped together across the upper thighs and chest. We used A-3 types with two pack fastening snaps, one on each side of the chest. Matching U-shaped projections on the chute pack would snap onto the harness snaps if it were needed. My chute pack went under the radio room desk, easy to reach. Under the tight harness the Colt began to dig a groove in my rib cage.

The flak vest, another potential life-saver, hung for now over the ammo box, under my parka. Plates of helmet metal, about one-by-two inches, fit into overlapping canvas pockets to provide flexibility and protection, we hoped. A chest section snapped to a shorter part over one's back. Another section attached below to cover the waist and crotch. It looked something like a baseball catcher's protector, except for its weight of at least 20 pounds. We used these ungainly shields only in flak or fighter areas.

Sitting finally at the radio desk I slipped into my leather helmet and snapped the strap with interphone mike buttons around my neck. Helmet earphones and mike cord jacked into the interphone lead. This put me back in touch with the rest of the ship and the world. Goggles stayed for now high on my forehead. The steel helmet, with hinged ear flaps that would accommodate the earphones in my leather helmet, still lay on the floor next to the makeshift chair. Three layers of gloves, nylon first, then heavy wool felt and finally, leather, turned my hands into awkward mounds.

The four gunners to the rear during this time dressed about the same, except for a lot of personal refinements. Nobody ordered what we'd wear, except for oxygen and interphone connections. The Army issued us the gear and assumed we'd use it, somehow. Nearly everybody ignored the heavy parka and insulated pants because of their great bulk.

Army Air Force manuals recommended that if one didn't have the new heated suit with shoes he should wear layers of heavy wool socks instead of shoes inside the sheepskin boots. But nearly all crewmen chose the GI shoes, just in case they had to bail out. Sheepskin boots usually flew off when a parachute opened, and nobody wanted to slog about Europe in socks alone. For the same reason, many ball and tail gunners who had to use the thin electric shoes for warmth, carried GI shoes along. When they dressed for a mission they tied their shoes to a loose metal snap. Then, if they had to bail out they'd clip them to their harness. Some put their shoes and other gear in a small bag which snapped to the harness whenever needed.

Almost everybody had added a woolen scarf, not government issue. These often appeared in bright colors, as did wool sweaters, usually worn under the heated suit. Tail gunners and engineers, exposed to brilliant sun in their positions, often sported caps with outrageously long bills. For extra protection from the sun nearly everybody adopted dark GI sunglasses. One stylish co-pilot wore a brilliant red tam-o'shanter even during missions.

Because pilots couldn't dress along the way and because of the heated flight deck they dressed before takeoff, and a bit lighter.

We had been up for half an hour so I switched the interphone control to "Liaison" and on the flight log recorded the first coded weather report from base. By now our group had formed and we had moved over to the coast to meet the three other groups. We'd lead the attack, so as they showed up in the next few minutes the other groups simply fell in line behind. We headed generally north in a steady climb, our indicated air speed hovering around 135. At this point we needed to gain altitude and to ration fuel more than we needed speed.

In this climb to altitude under full load engineers and co-pilots had to keep an eye on cylinder-head temperatures. When readings hit 200 degrees they could open cowling gills on the engines a bit to allow more air circulation. Opened too soon or too much, however, they simply added more air resistance and added to overheating. As a plane rose to colder temperatures the cowl flaps gradually had to be closed.

Pilots liked to synchronize the speed of all four engines and found that matching the strobe-effect "shadows" on the props was more accurate than the RPM gauges.

We hit 12,000 feet over the Adriatic and the bombardier told us to go on oxygen. I snapped the molded rubber mask to my leather helmet and plugged its short hose into the flexible six-foot line from the demand regulator. A strong spring gripper held the line to my coveralls so I wouldn't pull the hose loose in moving around the room. Using the mask also meant unplugging the throat mike and plugging in the mask mike. All of us in turn reported ourselves "on oxygen." Also, we had connected our heated suit cords to the plane's 12-volt electric system. I had removed my heavy gloves for easier writing in the log, but now the growing cold forced me back to them.

About now the pilot told the engineer to transfer fuel from the Tokyo tanks. These extra cells had been added starting with F models and lay in the B17's wings beyond the outboard engines. When readings in the six main tanks dropped to a certain level the engineer started electric pumps which transferred gasoline inward.

About the time we crossed the Yugoslav coast northwest of Split the pilot told us to test our guns. He and other pilots had spread the formation to make sure our spent rounds from the chin turret, the ball and tail didn't hit planes below and behind. I fired about 20 rounds from my gun and could hear a muffled banging throughout the ship. Tracers from upward-firing guns filled the part of the sky I could see. The smell of burned powder swept through the plane for an instant. All of us from nose to tail reported our guns OK. I kicked my own spent cartridges into a small pile and threw the flight bag on them to prevent their rolling around underfoot.

We passed west of Zagreb, Yugoslavia, and the navigator reported on interphone that we had climbed past 25,000 feet. Our air speed was now around 180. Frost started forming on metal in the plane and already I had lost communication with my big feet, always the coldest part of my body. Stomping on the plywood floor and kicking the bulkhead ahead of the desk did little to restore feeling. The electric suit had overheated my belly and left my back chilled. The pistol made my chest ache.

We passed Lake Balaton in Hungary at more than 28,000 feet and our indicated air speed had risen to 200. The pilot broke in to tell us to watch for fighters. I had just decoded the latest weather note, and stood up and switched my interphone lead to the cord on the gun. The plexiglass hatch in the top of the radio room, measuring about 2 1/2 X 5 feet, gave me a marvelous view above and behind. The sky had turned a sparkling dark blue. The bombardier and pilot could be seen clearly in the plane on our right wing, probably 75 feet above and behind. Vapor trails from several P38s lazily crossed our path far above. Behind us, almost hidden behind our own billowing trails, specks followed us in formation. Undoubtedly they were planes in one of the groups behind us.

Below, however, solid, silvery clouds now obscured what had been a clear view of the ground. I switched from "liaison" to "inter" and could hear the navigator and bombardier debating our chances of seeing the target. The navigator figured we had arrived in the target area. Within minutes the group leader started a sharp turn, or as sharp as 28 planes can make in formation. The turn continued until we had completed a circle, about 20 miles across. The bombardier speculated that we had simply given the other groups time to close up.

We made more turns and other B17 groups passed us on courses different from ours and at two or three miles distance.

"We're going home."

The stark message from the pilot over the interphone left me startled and confused. I had not been monitoring the "command" channel, but now assumed that our pilot and the rest of the group had received the word from our group lead. Once the formation had settled on a southerly heading the pilot confirmed my theory. Too many clouds to bomb visually, he said. We would carry our load home.

From interphone conversation one could feel the tension evaporate, despite the pilot's renewed caution that we watch for fighters. Within minutes the engineer reported a "One-Oh-Nine. High at three o'clock!" Tension flooded back. I twisted to look over my left shoulder and saw the gray fighter turning away, out of range. Probably only nosing around, the engineer assured us.

I became aware suddenly that the flak vest and steel helmet still lay unused. Under the circumstance my inattention seemed minor. In any case my stomach told me it was time to open the K-ration box. My watch indicated about 10:30 a.m., but breakfast now seemed a week away. The frost-covered oxygen mask had to be unsnapped for each bite of cold, salty eggs, skewered on the end of my pocket knife.

I decoded a weather report from base just in time. The pilot wanted to know what storms or clouds we'd find in our part of Italy. Fortunately, the front that now covered our target had not extended far to the south.

We crossed the eastern Alps, their snowy peaks visible through low clouds, and entered northern Italy. We started losing altitude, and my continued foot-stomping began to restore feeling to my toes. The ball gunner opened his hatch behind me and stood up, half out of his position. He unhooked his heat, interphone and oxygen lines, cranked his turret to bring the guns horizontal and came into the radio room. There he reattached his umbilicals and sat on the floor on the right side.

"Yo, Radio! How'd it go?"

He had unhooked his mask and yelled at me instead of using the interphone. The whole crew knew they had a beginner along.

"Not bad. Colder'n hell. What did we do?"

"Damned if I know," he yelled back. He shrugged the shrug of a forlorn, mystified GI and leaned back for a nap. This act of the uninformed, innocent participant pulled thousands of soldiers like him through most events they'd rather not try to understand. Anyway, the brass got paid to sort out our mysteries, or act as if they had.

We could see the water of the Adriatic now. Everybody yanked the heated suit plugs and a few minutes later went off oxygen. Both waist gunners and the tail gunner busily shed their extra gear in the waist and lay down. They had completed their duties for now.

None of the other groups could be seen as we turned west across the Gargano spur. Low box first, then Dog, Baker and Able squadrons peeled off from our formation as we crossed Amendola at a couple of thousand feet. I could hear our wheels going down and then our flaps, down a third of the way for the base leg and all the way as we lined up with the runway.

Planes landed in quick succession despite their bomb loads, which made them touch down a bit faster, maybe 125 mph. I switched off my receiver and transmitter while still on the runway. The co-pilot shut down the inboard engines, closed the turbo controls, opened the cowl flaps and raised the wing flaps. As we taxied I struggled out of my flying gear and stowed it in the bag. The pilot spun the tail around on the hardstand, gave the brakes a final, screeching touch and cut the two outboard engines. We had been gone six hours and 20 minutes.

I thrust a signed repair sheet into the hands of the ground crewman at the waist door. Grasping my flimsy in one hand and flight bag in the other, I climbed into a truck with the others. We soon dropped our bags at the crew shack and wheeled off to interrogation at group.

When we hopped off the trucks in the yard at group nearly everybody stopped for a doughnut and cup of lemonade at the Red Cross van. Flip Frame, a good-natured woman who appeared to be in her thirties, handed us our prizes with a cheerful greeting.

Nobody had much to say at interrogation since we hadn't made a bomb run. We did report the single fighter near the target. Intelligence folks told us that our old sister group, the 301st, had lost 11 planes to fighters while circling near Vienna. That jolted everybody, and especially me. The sky had looked so peaceful.

My radio log and flimsy went back to the folks at the group radio shack. Then, except for the two pilots those in the crew now returned by truck to the plane to clean our guns. This crew had adopted a drill for that process. Half the gunners disassembled and cleaned bolts inside the plane. The other half manipulated barrel cleaning rods while standing on the fuselage or ground, quickly swabbing and oiling at each position. Ground crews already had restarted engines to check their condition, and armorers had reloaded ammo boxes. We stuck an oiled cleaning patch in the muzzle of each gun barrel to protect it from the dust, then headed back to the squadron. We knew at least that we had saved work for the bomb loaders.

Our watches indicated only a little after 3 p.m. Flood, Tuck and Grove, who arrived at our tent about the same time as I, displayed the same weariness. We all collapsed on our cots until chow. After eating we showered to erase what appeared to be a week's grime. The flying list for the next day didn't include any of us, so in candlelight we sat and talked far into the evening. Our experiences that day had not made veterans out of neophytes, but we had learned a bit.

One lesson involved our Colt .45s. Each of us without comment packed that steel monster away in the bottom of a box or bag and forgot it.

Before blowing out my candle I found a notebook and started a section titled "Record of Missions:"

July 26--Weiner Neustadt, Germany:
109 motor factory--no bombs dropped because of clouds. No flak--one fighter. Time 0620. 11 ships of 301st shot down.

15. Hardening

Following is part of my letter home the day after that first mission:

> *Italy*
> *July 27, 1944*

> *Sorry I haven't written the last two days. We have finally been put to work and it sure keeps us on the go. . .*
> *Just think, it was nearly two years ago that Bob and I started school over at Wahpeton. . .*
> *Still see a show about every other night. Last night it was "Action in the North Atlantic" starring Humphrey Bogart. The "theater" is just one of the things here to it (sic) livable.*
> *Hall got a letter the other day, but so far I haven't had any mail at all. . .*

We visited the beach again that day and bought some melons. In the evening after chow we found our names on the flying list for the next day and, as expected, still scheduled with other crews.

In the briefing room the next morning the atmosphere turned somber as soon as we entered. Boistrous chatter that had occupied us on the path suddenly fell away to silence. My crew, the same one I had flown with two days earlier, had fixed their eyes on one word, chalked at the corner of the briefing room blackboard:

Ploesti.

After only two weeks with the outfit we had heard all the stories about this target: flak so heavy you could walk on it--that sort of thing. Eleven oil refineries surrounded this Romanian city that is about 40 miles north of Bucharest. Since 1940 these plants had supplied a good part of Germany's natural fuel for its war machine. In 1941 Germany's oil production had totalled 5.54 million metric tons, supplemented by 2.81 million tons of imports. Of the imported oil, 2.11 million tons had come from Romania. German troops had entered that country on Oct. 7, 1940, with the pretext of helping to reorganize the Romanian army, but Hitler's true concern had been to control the Ploesti oilfields and refineries.

Americans had made Ploesti a target as early as June 11, 1942, when 13 B24s led by Col. Harry Halverson flew from Cairo and dropped their bombs ineffectively before landing in Turkey, Syria and Iraq. Then on Aug. 1, 1943, five groups of B24s flying from Africa had carried out a daring but largely unsuccessful low-level raid on Ploesti refineries, losing 45 planes out of 177 that started.

In April, 1944, as the strategic bombing emphasis turned to oil, the 15th Air Force, including the 97th, returned to Ploesti. Our trip this day would be its 14th raid in that campaign. Ploesti flak defenses had been estimated the third most powerful in Europe, behind Berlin and Vienna, but among crews in the 15th Air Force, Ploesti gunners ranked at the top.

In charge of protecting the refineries, Lt. Gen. Alfred Gerstenberg had installed Wurzburg radar to direct the flak batteries. Two dummy Ploestis had been built, one eight miles to the northwest and one seven miles to the east. In addition to all the other guns, a train of 88 mm guns mounted on flatcars moved between the city and the town of Floresti. Hundreds of smoke pots could conceal targets within 20 minutes.

Our briefing officer repeated much of the information from the blackboard. Our target, the Americana Romana refinery, lay about 5,000 yards to the east of the city. A photo projected on our screen showed us our aiming point: a power plant in the midst of distillation units, and our briefing officer emphasized their importance over mere oil tanks and pipework. Each plane would carry a standard three tons of 500 pounders. Twelve groups would go after Ploesti targets on this day, so lead pilots and navigators had to observe strict headings, altitudes and release times.

After takeoff we formed without incident over the base and fell into line with other groups in our climb eastward over the Adriatic. Over the Albanian coast Fifth Wing groups took their places in a stream of other groups, mostly B24s that flew several thousand feet lower. In any direction one could see evidence of a major effort. P38s and P51s provided a comforting umbrella of essing trails as we crossed the Danube on Romania's southern border.

"Ten minutes to the IP."

I had been busy taking a weather broadcast from our base. The navigator's voice, breaking into all other positions on the interphone, startled me, but I tried to calm down as I snapped on the flak suit and found the steel helmet. Getting to my feet with some difficulty under the added bulk and weight, I opened the bomb bay bulkhead door and then plugged into the interphone cord at the gun.

On the bomb run the radioman had to check the bombs at "bombs away" and repeat those words to the bombardier if they had, indeed, dropped clear. If they failed to go out in the normal string he'd yell, "Salvo!" and the bombardier would dump them all at once, using another circuit. For now I pulled the goggles down over my sunglasses and studied the sky above and behind.

"Two minutes to the IP. Start dropping chaff."

The IP, or initial point, was an easily identifiable ground feature which marked the beginning of our four-minute bomb run. Already we had started a sweeping left turn so as to cross the IP on the right heading, and everything in the plane appeared to tighten as engines wound up to a hard, almost fierce, pitch. The right waist gunner began dropping loosely wrapped swatches of chaff, aluminum foil strips, through an opening near his gun position. The foil, about an eighth-inch wide and ten inches long, reflected enemy radar signals and, presumably, threw off range readings.

Black keyholes of smoke stitched across the sky, fixing my attention. A Seventeen in a group a mile behind and a little above us blew up. Unaccountably, the other planes around it continued without hesitation.

As the navigator yelled, "IP," the ship shivered just a bit, then came a harsh rattling up close and a muffled banging as if several people had slammed their car doors. Our bomb bay doors opened and a blizzard of frost swept around me. About 10 feet from my window our left wing showed small, jagged eruptions as black smoke from 88 mm bursts whipped over us. I could smell German gunpowder and saw at least 50 oily puffs between us and Charlie box, ahead and to our left.

The bombardier said "level" a couple of times and then, "We're OK." Nobody reported any fighters. Engines in two ships to our right and above in Baker Box trailed smoke.

"Bombs away!"

The plane surged upward as our load ticked loose, first a bomb from one side and then from the other. Surprised, I needed a second to control my senses and repeat, "Bombs away!" Then the bay doors closed and the bombardier yelled, "Left, left! Let's get the hell out of here!"

Flak appeared to follow us in volleys as our group spread out. We stayed in loose formation but each pilot took violent evasive action. The bombardier, trying to anticipate battery fire, helped direct us to more peaceful sectors of the sky. Streams of gray smoke seemed to come from planes everywhere around us and feathered props appeared in nearly every formation. Two ships dropped behind a group formation that passed about a thousand feet under us, and a handful of parachutes floated several miles away, close to the ground.

A sharp crash and thud behind me sounded as if someone had fallen, hard. Then the ball gunner announced almost calmly on the interphone that his turret wouldn't turn. The pilot asked if he was OK and said he had better leave his position. The group had completed a broad turn back to the west, its parts still weaving and dodging through bursts that had memorized our altitude. To me it seemed an hour since we hit the IP, rather than minutes.

Flak stopped as suddenly as it had started. Engine and ship sounds loosened as our two pilots eased controls away from combat power. As our formation closed up one plane shed a mist of fuel from a wing. Its pilots seemed to be trying to restart one engine. Switching to "Liaison," I heard the bomb drop report from the radio operator in the lead plane. It amazed me that the world still functioned despite the wrenching it had just experienced.

The crew reported "OK" in response to the co-pilot's query, even the ball gunner. With some difficulty he had managed manually to crank the elevation gears down so he could open his hatch inside the plane and get out. Everybody cautioned everybody else to watch for fighters, but nobody reported any so I retrieved my radio log from under the transmitter and recorded a weather report. Despite my numb hands and feet, despite the frost ringing my oxygen mask, sweat ran into my eyes. Off came the flak vest, steel helmet and goggles. Weak and shaky legs could hardly move my weight.

All that frenzy, a mixture of fear, tension and near-panic, in passing had left me limp and exhausted. My first contact with the enemy could not have pretended much success, but thankfully, that enemy, wherever he was, didn't know my terror or weakened condition.

Nothing could have prepared me for that day. Nothing, outside a life of brutishness, prepares anyone for action in war. No concentration of thought or imagination braces the senses for war's overwhelming truth: Somebody out there wants to kill you. And uncovering that stark secret doesn't dull its shock for the next day, or the next. I doubt that anyone, in any lifetime of battle, has erected effective mental breastworks against fear. Safety becomes an impostor, and most physical acts toward self-preservation simply keep one busy.

This time as squadrons approached the base at Amendola eight or ten planes ignored landing protocol and patterns. Low on fuel, carrying wounded crewmen or nursing damaged engines, they left formation and came straight in from the coast. They aimed almost instinctively for the nearest runway, two of them firing distress flares. Our tower folks held the rest of us in a wide circle until all the emergencies had cleared the runway. Ambulances, or "meat wagons," chased these planes to their hardstands.

As we gathered at benches outside the interrogation office a doughnut from the Red Cross van lay in my stomach like a small brick. Then searing warmth from a big shot of "Old Overholt" immediately dissolved effects of the doughnut. The intelligence officer told us more than we could tell him. Forty fighters had attacked one of our groups but had been driven off. That day our Air Force had dropped 913 tons of bombs and damaged six refineries. It had lost 20 bombers--200 men--in grisly payment for the battered plants.

Back at the ship to clean the guns we found that the ground crew already had started to repair damage. They had counted 16 holes, mostly in the left wing just behind a main tank. A big chunk of shell had hit the side of the ball turret, almost breaking it loose, but it would be easy to replace the 1,200-pound ball and its hanger, they assured us. The skin man already had cut aluminum rectangles of varying sizes to rivet over holes in the wing. One new radio operator had mixed feelings about their calm confidence, and about how even the meanest event pales under mundane work.

After showers and before chow that afternoon those in my crew related their experiences. It appeared that every plane in the group had reported damage. Nobody, including me, mentioned the fear, but that omission too seemed to be a part of war. The day, warm, bright and beautiful, washed away any remaining concerns. We decided to attend the movie that night.

After chow, a short letter home:

Italy
July 28, 1944

. . .Had another very busy day today. You can imagine what we were doing. Boy, I was never so scared in all my life. We'll get over that tho. . .

There is a nice cool breeze blowing now. I just had a shower and feel pretty good. Tired, tho . . .Everybody but Flood and I got letters today. I'm looking for a bunch tomorrow. . .

I broke my watch today. Will get a new one tomorrow. . .

The mission notation in my notebook that night:

July 28--Ploesti Rumania:
Americano-Romano oil refinery. Believed to have damaged it. Very heavy flak. All ships damaged. We had 16 holes and ball turret put out of commission. Saw a 17 blow up in group behind us. Time--0815.

16. More Breaking In

After a day off, and still with another crew, I flew on a one-group mission to hit a railroad marshaling yard in Brod, Yugoslavia. We had briefed for a target in Budapest but at the last minute the wing leader diverted us to this alternate or secondary objective. Hitting rail yards like this one made great hash out of German army supply efforts on the Eastern front, so we did our bit for the Russian army.

July 30, 1944—Brod, Yugoslavia. (Secondary)
Hit marshaling yards. Moderately heavy flak,
but not accurate. 0620.

The pilot of this crew made the six hours and 20 minutes seem like a week as a result of overcontrol. Generally speaking, good element and squadron leaders made formation flying easy. Most pilots and co-pilots handled their controls smoothly, without much apparent strain. Pilots and co-pilots would agree in advance on a schedule for relieving each other at the controls. This time we flew on the right wing of the lead in Dog Box, so having the best view of the lead, the pilot would have done most of the flying, his eyes glued to the squadron leader. The pilot not at the controls kept his eyes on the sky and the instruments. He also stayed in contact with the crew by intercom.

Although manuals cautioned against it, pilots often kept inboard engines at a constant rpm and maintained position in formation by jacking the outboard throttles forward or backward a quarter inch at a time. Some pilots asked their co-pilots to adjust the rpm, and vice-versa, depending on which had the controls. Adjusting the turbo knobs probably served best in keeping a plane in position.

This pilot on the mission to Brod overran his lead plane about once every two minutes. Overcompensating, he'd ease the throttles back, pull the nose up and alternate between the rudder pedals to reduce speed. We'd fishtail for a minute and fall back too far. Reacting by pushing the throttles ahead too much, he'd start the overrun process all over again. We rode this miserable roller coaster all the way to the target and back. During our ride to interrogation that afternoon the engineer said he liked his pilot but thought that the crew deserved a special medal.

Part of a letter home that afternoon:

Italy
July 30, 1944

Taking it easy this afternoon--sure was sweating this morning, tho.

It rained last night, and we were running around patching the tent and trying to keep dry.

Visited Foggia not so long ago. It isn't much of a place to try to enjoy yourself. . .

Guess you know your son is now a Sgt. . .

You might save these letters. May want to reminisque (sic) a little sometime. You can probably keep up with what we are doing by keeping track of the 15th Air Force. . .

Clearly, though Skok still read our letters before we dropped them in the squadron mail box, restrictions had eased on what we could write in them. Our new rank had come as a formality because we had started flying in combat. Engineers and radio operators got promotions a step at a time until they were Technical Sergeants, and gunners advanced to Staff Sergeants.

Next day I flew again to Ploesti, still with another crew. This time we plastered the Standard Oil refinery on the south edge of the city. During the bomb run we passed through flak even more accurate than before. A chunk apparently hit one of the bombs and smashed into bits, spraying between my body and my right arm, which I had raised to control the interphone button on the gun. The fragments wiped out one of the tuning units on the back wall.

Two planes blew up in a group in front of us, the only losses from the mission, which involved 154 aircraft. Again, several planes trailed smoke, some dropping out of formation. I knew from the sound that flak had hit us several times. Twenty five planes in our group reported damage, and four men were wounded.

We ran into another example of poor flying on this mission, this time by leaders of other groups. Twice, once as we turned to approach the IP, and once as we left the bomb run, other groups turned across our course in front of us, out of position. It caused a lot of swearing and consternation in our group as squadron leaders frantically took defensive action. After we landed the exasperated pilot told us that inexperienced group and wing leaders caused the problem. Given a time schedule for starting a bomb run, but failing to arrive on time, they'd try to swing in ahead of other groups and thereby risk the whole operation.

No pilot could lead the 97th, we learned, until he had flown enough to know how to get a group to its target on time. He also had to master that big turn into the IP, to hit it on the specified bomb-run heading. Too many group leaders couldn't identify initial points until they were on top of them. Too many flew directly to the IP, then started the turn. Because a group in formation turned something like a battleship, that invariably threw it beyond the correct course. By the time an errant group swung back on the bomb line, little or no time remained for the group bombardier to line up on target. This sometimes forced the leader to make a "three sixty," a complete circle, to return for another bomb run. That of course invited a fury of flak and disastrous encounters with other groups at the same altitude.

Part of a letter that night:

July 30, 1944

Well, another hard day. Sure get tired when they don't give us a day in between to rest. . .

Still haven't had any mail. . . Flood says I should strike up an aquaintance with someone who can write. . .

Lasota is getting disgusted. He's been going for the last ten days. Sure going after that oil. . .

We had fresh plums last night--from some local farm, I guess. . .

This notation went into the little book that night:

July 31--Ploesti Rumania:
Standard Oil Refinery--hit good and hard.
Intense and accurate flak. Ball and top turret hit,
bomb bay, & both wings. Over 20 holes in ship.
Large piece of flak hit a bomb and sprayed past
me, one passing between my chest & arm. Two
ships blew up in front of us. 0740

And so ended the month of July. The 15th Air Force
had lost 318 heavy bombers during the month, the highest
monthly loss it would ever sustain. In fact, the 15th had recorded more casualties in July than the total reported by the
Fifth and Eighth ground armies combined. Groups at this
time often lost planes and crews equal to their full complement in less time than it took for a crew to complete its 50
missions. Losses reflected a conscious shift to oil targets.
One encouraging development: The 306th Wing, the seven
groups of fighters who protected us, had proven its effectiveness. Pilots of our 51s and 38s reported they had shot
down over a thousand German fighters since the wing formed on April 2.

Old timers could see a weakening of enemy fighter
strength even though German production of new fighters
actually had increased, from 5,515 in 1942 to 25,285 in
1944. Two developments, however, the loss of experienced
pilots and a growing shortage of aviation fuel, made it
impossible for the Luftwaffe to use its new planes effec-
tively.

Introduction of the P51B as an escort fighter for
bombers had changed the air war considerably soon after
the beginning of 1944. Command of the air over Germany
had begun to swing decisively to our side as early as February and March, mostly because of the 51s. In October,

1943, the Army Air Forces lost 9.1 percent of their bombers. By March, 1944, bomber losses totalled 3.5 percent.

Equipped with Rolls Royce Merlin engines, P51s could hit 455 mph in an emergency at 30,000 feet. Using two 108-gal. disposable drop tanks they could fly 1,500 miles. This enabled them to escort bombers all the way to the most distant targets, which P38s and P47s couldn't do. Even more important, pilots on both sides said they outperformed both the Messerschmitt 109 and the Focke Wulf 190, Germany's best fighters.

Even P51s couldn't fly for eight or nine hours, however, so fighter units normally shared the work. Some flew cover for specified bomb groups during approach to the target. Others flew cover over the target, and still others covered bombers on the first hour or so after leaving the target.

By July, when our crew arrived, German interceptor groups succeeded only by pouncing in masses on single groups or on stray planes. They especially favored attacking single strays that had lost an engine or two. We sometimes encountered twin-engine ME 110s or JU88s, trying to lob rockets at our formations from about 1,000 yards off. Their missiles flew erratically and rarely hit anything. Accuracy of German air-to-air rockets reportedly improved by the spring of 1945.

The Luftwaffe has been described as a mixture of brilliance and confusion. Adolph Hitler's misguided leadership caused many of its problems throughout the war, turning it by 1944 into a magnificent failure. Germany's scientists had developed several new planes and other weapons which could have threatened our bombing effectiveness, but Hitler scotched them.

The ME262, a remarkable two-engine jet fighter, for example, received production priority in January, 1944. It had flown at 660 mph and could have replaced the ME109, the first models of which had flown in 1935. For some months in 1944 allied military leaders feared that the ME262 could regain control over German skies. But Hitler ordered his designers to make them into bombers. Except for one experimental unit of 30 fighters, his order removed the ME262 from combat.

Germany had a good ground-to-air rocket ready for mass production in the fall of 1944, according to Hitler's war production chief, Albert Speer. The 25-foot Waterfall carried a warhead of 660 pounds and might have devastated our bomber formations. Hitler, not fervently interested in defensive systems, vetoed the project.

The Luftwaffe developed and used a piloted rocket in 1944, but without much effect. A Walter rocket engine propelled the ME 163 Komet at 600 mph, and it carried a cannon, but only enough fuel for 12 minutes of engine use before having to glide to a landing. The little thing burned a dangerous mixture of hydrazine hydrate and methyl alcohol. We saw a few of these over southern Europe. Komet pilots used their engines in bursts to save fuel and left a tell-tale line of white dashes across the sky. They'd zoom past us going up, then zoom past going down. Few scored any hits.

A decreasing threat from German fighters didn't mean that we owned the skies. About 12,000 heavy and 30,000 light flak guns defended the inner Reich. Half of the heavy guns and a fourth of the light ones defended oil plants. Flak, not fighters, caused more than 90 percent of the 55,000 reports of battle damage to our heavy bombers in 1944. Germany had 1,250,000 personnel assigned that year to anti-aircraft work, including combat units.

Heavy anti-aircraft guns firing at us included 88 mm, 105 mm and 128 mm pieces. The 88s, probably the best gun developed on either side before and during the war, caused us more grief than any other weapon because of its accuracy. Germans used it against us in the air, as ground artillery and as the big gun in the Tiger tank. An 88 mm shell, which weighed about 20 pounds, could wreck any plane, even when exploding at a distance. German gunners aimed their batteries with optical sights in daylight and clear weather. Working under clouds or at night they aimed their guns from radar data.

We used chaff to create clutter on their radar screens and also radio jammers that covered their radar frequencies. One plane in each of our groups carried transmitters that automatically and constantly varied their frequencies over the German radar spectrum. The radio operator on that plane monitored enemy radar signals and, finding one, locked another transmitter's frequency onto it to spoil its reception.

We would have towed a lead balloon if we had thought it would help. We defended ourselves best against German flak batteries by avoiding them. Fifth Wing planners made a fetish of carefully plotting courses to targets and over them to avoid as many guns as possible. Even more important, B17 groups rarely flew at less than 28,000 feet over heavily defended targets, and we often bombed from more than 30,000 feet. The accuracy, even of 88 mm guns, dropped off 50 percent for every 5,000 feet of altitude above 15,000 feet. At heavy flak targets we in B17s considered B24s, flying four or five thousand feet lower, to be our best protection.

A crewman/poet composed these words for the tune to "As Time Goes By:"

As Flak Goes By

You must remember this:
The flak can't always miss.
Someone has to die.
The odds are always too damned high,
As flak goes by.

And when the fighters come,
You hope you're not the one
To tumble from the sky.
You wish you were at home and sigh,
As flak goes by.

One-Tens and Two-Tens knocking
At the gate. Sky full of fighters,
What will be my fate?
Bombs don't go away--salvo, don't delay!
The target's passing by.

It's still the same old story,
The 8th gets all the glory,
But we're the ones to die.
The odds are always too damned high
As flak goes by.

Flood, left, and Kleiber outside our tent at Amendola, August, 1944

Flood, left, and the author, while our bivouac area was still dry.

B17, taxiing, its bomb doors half open. Note P51 at left.

B24, taxiing. Its ball turret retracted for landing, takeoff.

17. The Big Ass Bird

Every time we took off we relearned how much we owed the designers and builders of the B17. Few pilots or crew members faulted the plane, though a cranky engine or other part might stir our irritation. It responded to controls with a style that built respect and confidence among its crews. We don't readily assume human qualities in our machines, but still, a Seventeen flew as if it wanted to fly.

Even when conditions forced a pilot to abuse the engines, even when the enemy had torn great chunks from its wings and body, the Seventeen trimmed out and sailed on. At our age in 1944 we didn't "love" anything but women, but we sure admired our airplane.

The first one produced, which Boeing called a Model 299, rolled out of the Seattle plant on July 16, 1935. The Seattle *Times* called it a "Flying Fortress," a name that stuck, but only among Army Air Forces public relations people. I never heard crewmen call them anything but Seventeens. For that matter, ground and air crews didn't have much use for most publicity names like "Liberator," "Mitchell," "Marauder," "Lightning," or "Mustang." The British stuck us with such names as "Spitfire" and "Lancaster" only because few people knew a military designation for RAF planes.

Not that we weren't romantics, too. Some poet wrote these homespun lines, called "Sky Beauties," about the P38:

Oh, Hedy Lamar is a beautiful gal,
And Madeleine Carroll, too,
But you'll find if you query
A different theory
Amongst any bomber crew.
For the loveliest thing
Of which one could sing
This side of the heavenly gates,
Is no blonde or brunette
Of the Hollywood set,
But an escort of P38s.

Byron, Shelley and Keats
Ran a dozen dead heats,
Describing the view from the hills.
Of the valleys in May
When the winds gently sway
An army of bright daffodils.
Take the daffodils, Byron,
The wildflowers, Shelley,
Yours is the myrtle, friend Keats.
Just reserve me those cuties,
American beauties,
An escort of P38s.

Boeing built 6,981 B17s. Soon after the G Models appeared the company concentrated on making B29s. Douglas Aircraft made 3,000 B17s under wartime license and Lockeed Vega made 2,700. Each plane cost $238,070.

Records show that combat missions and accidents took a toll of about 4,750.

The B17's design, nine years old when we flew the plane, had undergone a multitude of changes, but mostly in the tail and fuselage. That magnificent wing remained essentially the same in ten years of production. The single Model 299 had 750 hp Pratt and Whitney engines, but all the rest carried R-1820 Wright Cyclones. The nine-cylinder R-1820 had been designed in the 1920s and its power rating gradually increased to 1200 hp because of wartime refinements.

Each engine had a General Electric turbosupercharger. A turbine mounted in the exhaust system compressed outside air to at least ground-level pressures and fed it to the engine's carburetor. The Cyclones turned Hamilton Standard constant speed three-bladed propellers. "G" models, appearing late in 1943, swung props with "paddle" blades, which retained their width at their ends to maintain the plane's ceiling and speed despite additions to its weight.

These internal combustion engines got their power from burning a mixture of 100 octane gasoline and air. Atmospheric pressure at sea-level is about 30 inches of mercury, the standard of measurement. But without a pressurizing system provided by the superchargers, or "turbos," engine power would drop off rapidly as natural pressure decreased with altitude. The turbos could be adjusted to supply air under pressure up to 46 inches to the carburetors and intake manifolds.

Because natural pressure decreases, the air supply to an engine becomes more critical than gasoline as altitude grows. In fact, above 15,000 feet, pilots usually opened a B17's throttles, which governed fuel being pumped to the cylinders, and controlled engine power by adjusting the turbo knobs. This practice also prevented cylinders from exploding if a turbo "ran away."

Each turbo knob/lever controlled a waste-gate in an engine exhaust stack, governing the amount of gases turning the turbine wheel. Marked settings on the controls would produce a specified number of inches of manifold pressure. "Full military power," which produced the Cyclone's 1200 horsepower rating, came from an open throttle, 2500 rpm, and 46 inches of pressure.

Nice as it was to have that power available, an engine couldn't take that kind of pounding for more than a few minutes at a time. Pilots adjusted power settings more often for fuel economy than for speed, which usually had a lower priority. They used full power for takeoffs with full load, for bomb runs and for emergencies. Actually, B17s could reach military power and around 300 mph air speed at 30,000 feet using a turbo setting of 41.5 inches.

Full power, without any wind, would get a fully loaded B17 off a hard runway in 3350 feet at sea level. A 20 mph headwind would reduce that takeoff run to 2300 feet. Lead pilots usually climbed to altitude with a power setting of 2300 rpm and 38 inches. That produced a climbing air speed of about 135 mph and would get a formation to 25,000 feet in about 65 minutes. In addition to engine fuel pumps, B17s had boost pumps, used for starting engines, for takeoff, and for over 15,000 feet.

Cruising to a target, lead pilots had a broad selection of power settings, resulting in practical air speeds anywhere from 150 to 200 mph. If target schedules and the enemy allowed, they usually chose the lower settings for better fuel economy. A setting of 2300 rpm and 38 inches would produce and air speed around 200 mph, but use 413 gallons of fuel an hour. A setting of 2150 rpm and 31.5 inches

125

would produce an air speed of 150 and use only 284 gallons an hour. Fighter escort planes, also saving fuel, usually cruised at between 200 and 250 mph.

The return half of a bombing mission, because of no bomb load and much lower fuel load, required much lower power settings. This was true especially when, an hour or so after the target, a formation started down in altitude. Carburetor fuel mixtures, set at "auto rich" for the earlier part of the mission, could go to "auto lean" below 20,000 feet.

Designed originally to carry five .30 or five .50 caliber machine guns, Seventeens, by the time they had evolved to the "G" model, bristled with 13 Browning .50s. Experience in early combat, much of it in the Pacific, dictated every change. Front windows on the flight deck became bullet-proofed. Sheets of armor steel, about half an inch thick, went in front of the instruments, behind pilots, in the ball turret and under the waist guns. Added guns, ammo and armor brought the gross weight of a combat ship to 36 tons.

A B17's wing span measured 103 feet, nine inches. With changes to the tail and tail gun position the plane grew in length to 74 feet, nine inches. Fully loaded, a Seventeen's tanks held 2,850 gallons of fuel.

It's almost impossible to compare two aircraft designs, mostly because their designers usually had different objectives in mind. Changing any bomber's design to improve one objective: speed, fuel load, bomb load or service altitude, will affect the other three. Adding more fuel capacity, for example, will allow greater range, but probably will force reductions in bomb weight, speed and/or altitude achieved. Designing to fly higher will reduce both range and bomb loads. Increasing bomb capacity also will reduce performance in the others.

With this in mind, designers plan a military plane to meet demands of those who try to foresee needs. Any completed design may favor one or more of the four elements more than the others. The government orders planes that deliver the optimum mix of performance closest to its needs. Other factors complicating this balancing act: defense, maneuverability, ease and speed of production, ease of maintenance and cost.

Seventeens filled our military requirements in Europe almost precisely as they developed during World War II. Its optimum use: to deliver three tons of bombs at 300 mph, 30,000 feet over targets 700 miles from its base. That range, from England and Italy, covered most of the military targets in Europe. Both bomb load and speed were more than adequate. That altitude assured delivery of bombs through the heaviest flak defenses.

B17s supplied other qualities beyond basic requirements. Throwing in its flying characteristics and innate toughness, for example, together with its 13 guns, it became a formidable offensive and defensive machine. The B29, developed during the war, could have done well in Europe, but bombing of Japan required its greater range in that theater of the war.

Other bombers gave up one or more advantages in order to deliver greater bomb loads or range. The British built their Lancaster, for example, around a huge bomb bay. Whenever it carried ten tons of bombs it rarely flew at altitudes over 10,000 feet or for long distances. It could carry four tons of bombs to Berlin from England, but could reach only 22,000 feet. This altitude limitation forced its crews to fly at night, which reduced bombing accuracy dramatically. The B24 if necessary could carry fuel in one of its bomb bays, increasing its range but in exchange reducing its bomb load. Even carrying a normal load of three tons of bombs, the B24 could scarcely climb to 25,000 feet.

The Twenty four's assets gave it a definite edge in the Pacific theater where planes needed range and where Japanese defenses didn't require our planes to fly high. In Europe, however, daylight bombers had to seek every possible foot of altitude. B24 pilots, trying to climb above 23,000 feet, found their controls mushing up and their tails dragging low. An unstable, wallowing plane didn't engender much confidence among crews, especially in formation.

Beyond these general differences, comparisons between 17s and 24s dealt mostly in preferences among pilots and crews. Twenty fours had a couple of advantages: the nose wheel allowed them better maneuverability in taxiing, and their boxy fuselage gave crewmen more space.

While electricity powered most B17 systems, requiring only a few lines gathered along the fuselage, hydraulics provided energy for B24 systems. Piping which carried hydraulic fluid seemed to fill every foot of their wall space. Hit by gunfire or flak, even one of these pressurized lines could fill the ship with mists of oily red fluid. Crewmen learned to carry little wooden cones along for plugging broken lines. Ruptured tubes caused systems to fail. We saw B24s with at least one wheel and strut hanging down on nearly every mission.

Pilots who had flown both planes without exception preferred Seventeens for their easier, speedier control, their lift and stability. Much lateral B17 control came from mild use of ailerons, while B24 pilots pushed rudder pedals for the same kind of movement.

A pilot had to be pretty sloppy to get in trouble with a Seventeen. In a stall they'd fall off directly forward, and had to be forced into a spin. One pilot said he flew a B17 but had to drive a B24. Accounts of the air war repeatedly tell of B17s returning as far as 500 miles on two engines. One finds little evidence that a B24 could do that. Maybe that explains why our crews stood by their planes.

We learned that we could identify B24 fields from the scalped trees off the ends of runways. Twenty fours had a Davis high-speed wing, which helped give the plane about a 5 mph advantage over the B17 at full power, but didn't provide a surplus of lift at takeoff. The B17 had a wing area of 1,420 sq. ft., and the B24 wing totalled 1,048 sq. ft. The B24's high-speed wing needed more velocity for both lift and stability, which meant that it couldn't cruise smoothly at low speeds and save fuel while climbing.

In traditional military spirit, crews from the Fifth Wing ragged B24 crews mercilessly when we met them in town. Somebody even composed a little ditty to sing in the bistros to the tune of "Strawberry Roan":

Oh, those Bee-Dash-Two-Fours,
Oh, those four-engined whores,
The crews that fly in them
Must certainly lose,
At forty four inches
They won't even cruise,
Oh, those Bee-Dash-Two-Fours. . .

Forty four inches of manifold pressure from the turbos came from a pretty high power setting which, of course, shouldn't be necessary for cruising.

In our more profane moments we called our own ships "Big Ass Birds" because of the grand insolence of that vertical stabilizer. Perhaps to mimic us, and perhaps in derision, German defenders called the B17 "Der Gross Arse

Vogel." No plane awed a fighter pilot, but Jerry flyers said that going after a Seventeen was like trying to grab a porcupine.

One little ditty sung at post-mission parties gave credit to the plane's toughness:

Just give me a B17.
They call her the four-engine queen.
She'll creak and groan,
But she'll bring me back home.
Just give me a B17.

The plane's only weakness in early European combat had been against fighter attacks from directly in front, just under the fire of top turret guns. German fighter pilots discovered and exploited this weakness in both B17s and B24s. Designers soon found ways to install turrets in the noses of both. Consolidated designed its own turret for the Twenty Four, and Bendix produced a "chin" turret for the B17G, remotely operated by the bombardier, who sat on top of it.

Adding the chin turret should have prompted removal of the two cheek guns operated by the navigator, but most groups kept them. Logically, builders could have discarded those two guns, the radio room gun and the two waist guns without seriously damaging the plane's defenses. It would have reduced the crew by two and removed more than a ton of armor, guns and ammo. Especially after the summer of 1944, the three turrets and twin tail guns could have furnished more than enough firepower in all directions. I always considered the top turret most effective, then the tail guns, the chin turret and ball turret in that order.

From the beginning, group leaders had found identification of other allied formations frustrating. So as early
as 1942 groups started painting identifying marks on their
planes. Within a year air commands had formalized this
practice to include wing, group and even squadron markings. In the 15th Air Force, for example, all Fifth Wing
planes carried a big "Y" on their vertical stabilizers.

Individual groups provided a background of differ-
ing shape and color. The "Y" on planes of the 97th appeared in black on a white triangle. Below the serial, black
numbers, 0, 1, 2, or 4, appeared in round, white spots to
designate the squadron. Tails in the 2nd Bomb Group carried white "Y"s in white rings. Those in the 301st carried
black "Y"s in white squares. The 99th placed a white "Y" in
a black diamond. The 463rd's white "Y" appeared in a
black, pie-shaped background, and the 483rd carried a black
"Y" without background. The 2nd, 463rd and 483rd groups
in addition painted rudders and elevators in prescribed colors.

Fighter groups, especially by 1944 when both the
allies and Germans dropped most efforts at aerial camouflage, adopted almost circus-like color schemes. They adorned their noses and tails in bright hues and designs often
extending halfway along the fuselage. The 332nd group of
P51s, flown by black pilots, displayed red tails. Based near
Cattolica, they often escorted the 97th. Another group of
51s which frequently escorted us carried black-and-yellow-
checkered tails.

Group and squadron markings had no connection
with the creative names and imagery daubed on the sides of
B17 nose sections. Such prosaic matters as repair schedules
and efficiency prevented an air crew like ours from flying all
its missions in a single plane. But even in 1944, when bom-

bing missions had become more matter-of-fact, sentimentality demanded spates of christening by paintbrush.

Imagination and artistic talent alone limited their design and extent. Women, both buxom and beautiful, predominated and blended most often with threatening and profane military themes. Had all of these promises been kept, we'd have ended the war much sooner. The practice of adding a bomb symbol to a plane's nose after every mission collapsed early in the game, along with any romantic illusions about flying over Germany.

These artistic displays extended to the leather jackets of air crewmen. Artists in any squadron would copy their best nose art on the backs of jackets for a price. In addition, some crewmen bought round leather squadron emblems which they sewed to the jacket's left breast, above the pocket. A month before we arrived in Italy the squadron had approved an official emblem: A Disney-created depiction of a frightened brown puppy, sitting on a damaged B17's tail. Artists had based it on a 414th plane, the "All American," which a German fighter had torn up in a collision the year before.

18. 'Maggie'

Italy
August 1, 1944

> *. . .Just reading in the "Stars and Stripes"*
> *for this area about what we did yesterday. Also read*
> *about it being so dry and hot in the Middle West. . .*
> *Haven't had any mail yet you know.*
>
> > *Will probably be busy tomorrow so will go*
> *to bed early. On nights when there isn't a show we*
> *hit the sack before nine. On days we don't fly, we*
> *just lay (sic) around and read. Oh yes, we also have*
> *our turn at guard duty. Haven't had to yet, however.*

Aside from our swimming breaks and an occasional foray into Foggia, our daily routines stirred little excitement. The squadron had started a little paper-back library in one end of the mess shack and Special Services distributed new titles every week or so. Without the reading our inactivity would have been hard to bear. Some ground crewmen, more practiced in the art of self-entertainment, worked on liberated Italian or German vehicles, causing their tents to look and smell like garages, but the mechanics avoided boredom.

Typical combat entrepreneurs from the squadron showed up at our tent one day with some pistols that had been confiscated from prisoners. They displayed several Walther P38s and little .32 cal. Berettas in holsters. Flood and Grove bought P38s but, remembering my trouble with the .45, I chose a Beretta and paid $20 for it in occupation scrip, which we used for all our purchases in Italy. The little pistol would fit comfortably in a shin pocket of my coveralls during missions and I could forget it. We bought several extra clips of ammunition and tested our new armament against cans in a nearby quarry, but marksmanship remained an elusive dream.

On the second of August five of us in the crew delivered a plane to Foggia Main field and left it for some special repairs. We caught a truck back to Amendola. Those kinds of freighting flights, like slow-timing new or overhauled engines, required only the two pilots, the engineer, navigator and radio operator. I assume that the navigator and I rode along only because of the possibility of getting lost in bad weather.

My long-awaited mail finally arrived on August 2.

Italy
August 2, 1944

I knew it would happen. I got nine letters today. Seven from you, one from Bob, and one from Aunt Ella. . . Old N. Dak. don't (sic) seem so far away when you can get letters. . .
Tell G'Pa there's no chance of me not keeping my earphones on. I had them on for 9 hours yesterday. On the way back, we usually tune in some news and hear about what we just did. You probably hear about it before we land. . .

Am going to take as many pictures as I can around here. Can get them developed in town. . . .

I referred to my brother in these letters as "Bob." His middle name was Robert, the one we used when we were kids. After the war he used his first name, John.

Finally scheduled together as a crew, we briefed on Aug. 3 for a chemical plant at Friedrichshaven, Germany, across Lake Constance from Switzerland. Near the target our wing leader diverted us to a secondary target, the Manzell aircraft factory which made ME 262 jet fighters.

Everything went smoothly. Squadron Operations folks had lent us a navigator and bombardier, two who stayed with us for most of our missions. The navigator, named Block, no longer had a crew of his own and already had completed two tours. A Jew, he said he knew of no better way to contribute to the war effort. Wolf, the bombardier, had lost his crew, whose plane had gone down one day when he wasn't with them. These two men made excellent replacements for Milburn and Grayson, and added some welcome experience to a pretty green crew.

Part of a letter home that night:

Italy
August 3, 1944

Got two letters from you, one from Bob and one from Bert today. This is more like it. Your last (sent Air Mail) was mailed the 26th, so it only took 8 days. Pretty fast--I guess Air Mail is best. . . .

The mission record:

135

August 3--Friedrichshaven, Germany.
Aircraft factory (secondary) some good hits.
Little flak and inaccurate. Two ships turn into
Switz. 0645.

The planes flying into Switzerland came from one of
the groups that attacked the chemical factory. They reported to their group leader that they had a lot of damage and
would try to land in the neutral country. Switzerland offered cushy asylum to "belligerents" during the war, so we
couldn't help but suspect a crew's motives whenever this
happened.

Part of a letter to my brother the next day:

Italy
August 4, 1944

. . .We get some pretty rough jobs here.
Some are so hard we get credit for 2 on them. Jerry
is tough and smart, but we're getting that way too.
Say, Mom says you've been roughing it last mo.
Kinda like we're doing I guess. I slept on a stretcher
for a week. . . .

The 15th Air Force until then had required air crewmen to complete 35 missions for a tour, but had changed
that requirement to 50. The new rules didn't make much
sense. Some missions, apparently determined arbitrarily by
star-dusted leaders in Bari, now counted as two, and others
counted only once. Credit had little connection with the
amount of opposition or general peril, and the change
caused a lot of cynicism among the crews. It seemed to
most of us that our leaders in wartime spent millions trying

to build the morale of servicemen, only to dump it coldly through crass decisions like this one.

Part of a letter home:

Italy
August 5, '44

>*. . .(the Italians') homes are pretty dirty because the towns were wrecked pretty much. They say Rome is nice and clean and modern. Want to go there if I can. . . .*
>
>*I have 75 dollars now (in scrip) and will be paid again in a few days. Will see if I can't send it home by money order. Laundry, haircuts and rations is (sic) all we buy here. Every once in a while we buy grapes, onions, eggs, melons from some farmers. Skok bought four small canteloupe for 200 lira ($2) the other day.*
>
>*Haven't seen any pretty Italian girls yet, Pop. They say there are some in Rome. Some WACs over at Manfredonia.*
>
>*Some guys have a motorcycle outside and I can't hear myself think. Lots of Jerry equipment around.*
>
>*There are a lot of locusts in the trees here. The first time I heard one I thought it was an electric razor. . . .*

On August 6 we bombed a large railroad marshaling yard in the Rhone River valley south of Lyons, France. Nothing unusual about it except that we all knew it was part of our preparation for an expected invasion of Southern France.

August 6--Portes les Valence, France. Wiped out an enormous marshaling yard. No flak at all. 0740.

Part of a letter that night:

Italy
August 6, 1944

Another busy day for us. It was a good day tho because we accomplished something. . .

It's trying to rain again tonite as every night lately. . .

. . .We will be busy again tomorrow, so will go to bed early tonite. Got up at 1:30 this a.m.

Next day we went all the way to the Oder River valley in Silesia. Half a dozen synthetic oil plants within a 25-mile circle had attracted our strategic planners and would keep us busy into the winter. Our choking off of outside oil supplies had forced Germany to revise its plans. Crude oil refineries now produced only 26 percent of its oil products, and synthetic oil, based on coal, accounted for the rest.

The Germans used two separate synthetic processes, Bergius hydrogenation and Fischer-Tropsch, the first being most important. As early as the first quarter of 1944 they supplied about 47 percent of all the Reich's oil products and nearly all its aviation fuel. The tie to coal concentrated synthetic refineries in the Ruhr valley near bituminous deposits and in Silesia near Germany's brown coal reserves.

Heavy air attacks of June, July and August caused German oil output to fall until in September it was only a tenth of that in May. Supplies of aviation gasoline had been hit even harder. By September production of airplane fuel had dropped off to 10,000 tons a month, contrasted to the Luftwaffe's minimum needs of 180,000 tons every month. This meant that Jerry fighters had to drink sparingly from reserves.

Even by the time our crew arrived in Italy, some 120,000 laborers worked at repairing damaged oil plants. This made repeated attacks necessary because a bombing might halt operations for only six weeks. Most of this anti-oil campaign fell to the 15th Air Force, because from May through August, Gen. Eisenhower had used the 8th Air Force tactically, first to prepare for the Normandy invasion, then for interdiction and to support our breakout efforts.

> **August 7--Blechhammer, Germany. Aviation gas plant. Some good hits. Twenty-mile flak barrage, but not accurate in our group. Was potted by flak battery in Yugo. Hall knocked over by hit on his flak vest. 30 holes. 0830.**

German gunners on this day introduced us to "box barrages." They apparently calculated where a formation would be and several batteries of 88s fired at that spot. It proved pretty deadly to the formations aimed at, but those nearly always proved to be low groups. On our way home over Yugoslavia an uncharted flak unit hit us in the waist area. Al Hall, trying to sleep, flipped head over heels when a chunk of flak hit his vest and chute harness. The hit on his harness near the shoulder expanded the webbing to football size, but left Hall with only a bruise and a case of nerves.

On this day also we met "Maggie," a plane which from this point we flew more than any other. Her full name was "Magnetic Maggie," painted in blocked orange letters on her right cheek. Explaining the name, her ground crew chief told us an earlier air crew had been impressed by the number of times she had attracted flak. She impressed Skok and Mabie by her neat trim-out, and she impressed all of us by bringing us home every time. Squares and splotches of bright aluminum marked patches that justified her name. We tended to call her "Zero-seven-one" from her serial.

I received my first package from home that day.

Italy
August 7, 1944

> . . .*Well, another busy day for us. A long ride, but it was worth it. Sure tired tonite. . .*
>
> *It rained a little again this afternoon before we got back. These roads are sure a mess. . .*
>
> *Had boiled Spam (sliced), stew, peas, 2 peach halves, cold cocoa & bread for supper tonight. . .really eat a lot. . .The water here has a lot of chlorine (halazone) in it, but tastes good when it's cold. . .*
>
> *Boy, I think I ache all over. Sure hard on a guy's nerves. . .*

In Normandy the next day Gen. Montgomery ordered U.S. and British forces to drive north and south, respectively, to complete encirclement of German armies in the Falaise area.

Italy
August 9

. . .Am taking life easy. Didn't get up til seven-thirty this morning, so had a good rest.

Went to town yesterday afternoon. Got some coffee and do-nuts at the Red Cross, got a crystal for Flood's watch, and looked at the rubble and ruin. A pretty dirty place. May go to the beach today if nothing comes up for us to do. . .

After all of this, I think I'll be glad to throw groceries. Boy what a life this is. Was actually glad to get back to the group last night. . .

Sure wish you could see this country. You wouldn't like it, but it's different. . .

We usually thumbed a truck ride into Foggia and headed for the Red Cross-sponsored enlisted man's club in the former City Hall, which GIs called "Duffy's Tavern." In addition to coffee we could get information about special activities and pass messages to other GIs through the bulletin board. A theater in town occasionally featured traveling plays and road shows for the troops. We saw Katherine Cornell and Brian Aherne one evening in "The Barrets of Wimpole Street."

We returned to Ploesti on August 10 and wrecked the Astra Romana oil refinery.

August 10--Ploesti, Rumania. Austro-Romano oil refinery. Very good bomb pattern on target. Smoke up to 25,000 ft. Could see it for 250 miles. Ship on our left wing burned--Pilot held ship level while nine men got out. Ship finally exploded--pilot aboard. Flak intense and very accurate. One straggler was attacked by 8 ME109s, but because of violent maneuvering by

**its pilot, was able to shoot down two of them &
return home. 0745.**

The entire Fifth Wing had flown a track that passed
south of Ploesti as if headed for Constanta on the Black
Sea. We had passed Bucharest about 30 miles when the lead
group turned sharply back northwest toward the target. The
maneuver outsmarted the defenders who had turned off
their smoke pots when they figured we had by-passed them.
Bomb-strike photos showed that smoke generators had started again but their gray clouds had not covered the target.

I wished that I had brought my camera along for that
one. A plane in Charlie position in the element ahead of us
dropped back beside us during the bomb run, its entire right
wing on fire. Men dropped out of the nose, bomb bay, waist
and tail as we watched. Nearly all of them made the mistake
of opening their chutes immediately. The abrupt stop snapped them cruelly. Within a minute their plane swung away
to the left and blew up. In all, our group lost two planes at
the target.

The pilot of the straggler on the way home put on a
grand flying exhibition. We could only watch and cheer. He
had only three engines going but he wrung that ship out for
about 15 minutes while the fighters attacked. He'd pull it up
in a stall, then dive to one side or the other, make a fast turn
or two, then stall it again. The sky around that besieged B17
filled with .50 Cal. tracers and with exploding 20 mm shells
from the fighters. The Jerry shells, set to go off at a terminal
distance so they wouldn't explode on the ground, looked
like sparklers. Two of the Messerschmitts pulled away,
smoking. It appeared to me that the B17's guns outranged
the German cannon. Our planes couldn't out-dive a fighter,
but without a bomb load and above 30,000 feet, we could

out-climb many fighters of the time. This Seventeen landed only a few minutes after we pulled onto our hardstand. Other crews at interrogation that day reported seeing two yellow parachutes, the color Jerry commonly used.

Italy
August 10

Rough day today. Boy, I feel as tho I'm broken in two someplace. Wasn't much physical work, but quite a strain on the nerves. Was really "sweating it out."

Cooled off quite a bit this afternoon because of the rain, so we can enjoy ourselves tonite, just sitting around--if the mosquitos don't run us out. . .

Somebody decided that our formations had become sloppy, a dirty word in the 97th. On the 12th the group flew two 2-hour practice missions up and down the Adriatic. We who flew could hear a lot of bossing from the lead plane:

"Come on, Baker Box! Close it up!"

As usual, bombardiers and gunners had a holiday.

Italy
August 12

Another day off, but I've worked pretty hard all day--just practicing.

Sure hot around here these days. We must drink gallons of water trying to keep cool. . .

Had roast beef, boiled potatoes, peas, gravy, bread, and grapefruit juice for supper. Every once in a while they really feed us here.

"Magnetic Maggie," sitting on a hardstand at Amendola in '44.

19. Interlude in Eden

August 14—We fly secretly to base at Bastia, Corsica, in preparation for invasion of southern France the next morning. Very short fighter runway and we burn up tires landing—also sink into mud at end of runway. We refuel, eat, go swimming in mountain pool, go to little French town, brief, and go to bed early. 0350.

Among all the bomb groups in Italy, only the 97th flew to Corsica on the 14th. In doing so we gained a jumping-off position more than half way to the invasion beaches. We used a strip made for a group of P38 recco planes, and I suspect that our colonel had made a deal with the boss of the P38 group. To support the invasion between 7:30 and 8 a.m., groups flying from their bases in Italy had to form up in the dark. Nobody liked to do that. In Corsica the 97th could take off just before dawn and form in the first light of day.

We landed hot on the short strip because of our bomb and fuel loads and had to use a lot of braking. Anyway, someone had foreseen our problems in dealing with the short, steel mat runway. Each plane in addition to its regular load carried an extra tire and a mechanic, but only half a dozen or so needed tire changes. Tugs retrieved our Seventeens from the mud.

We had flown to this strip on the northeast coast of Corsica in mid-morning. After getting some chow we went to explore the hills to the west. Burned-out Jerry tanks, overcome by French troops a few months earlier, still hung on the sides of the coastal road.

We walked through countryside not a bit like that around our base in Italy. Little valleys separated strikingly beautiful hills within a mile or two of the strip. Finding a small stone reservoir in the side of one hill, we stripped down for a dip that turned our lips blue in a minute. We dried off sitting in the sun on the pool's stone rim and from our perch picked ripe peaches from adjoining trees. Our bare bodies added to a perception that surely we had discovered Eden.

But we had to get back to the real world, so after dressing again we circled back to a coastal road where a couple of Jeep drivers gave us a lift into Bastia. Preparations for a major invasion had turned a normally sleepy coastal town into a wild mass of confusion, or so it seemed to us. We couldn't even get close to a bistro to buy some wine, so we caught a ride back to the strip.

Col. Nils Ohman, soon to take group command, was to fly his first mission with us and sat in on the briefing in the tent where we ate that evening. We sat at typical chow-tent benches beside one-star and two-star generals. We couldn't blame the brass at wing HQ for wanting to see an invasion as much as we did. In any case, none of us would ever get any closer to these folks who organized our fate.

We never got to thank our hosts. Somebody had put up extra tents and cots for nearly 300 of us. The briefing officer had told us our only concern on the mission would be the takeoff, so we went to bed early and slept like babes.

August 15—Hop off in the dark to bomb heavy gun installations at beachhead on Cape Camarat west of St. Raphael. Just 5 min. before barges landed the troops. Got to see huge invasion force in operation. Return to Amendola. 0530.

We pulled onto the strip pointing north, following two other planes in the lead box. Beyond the short runway barrage balloons hung directly ahead over the harbor at Bastia. Skok ran up the engines until everything jumped and shuddered. When he let the brakes go the back of my seat gave me a long shove. As soon as our wheels left the mat he cocked us over to the right in a steep turn to avoid the balloons. Black water glistened only feet from our right wingtip. We formed up in daylight over Corsica's northern cape, the island itself still hidden in darkness.

We flew almost straight west then turned north and crossed our designated map IP at about 12,000 feet. Because of the low altitude assigned for the bomb run we didn't need oxygen. Our regard for enemy air opposition in this area had dropped so low that we didn't even dress for the occasion.

But the view. When the bomb bay doors opened I straddled the bulkhead threshhold, sitting with one foot on the catwalk, to see the show. Below us stretched an entire invasion armada as we headed north, parallel to the beach. Ragged rows of troop landing craft made wide vees like water bugs only half a mile from the shore. Their parents loitered two or three miles to the east. That much farther offshore, destroyers spun white trails in the sea, their guns covered in smoke. Even farther to the east a row of three or four old battleships, barely moving, blasted at coastal defenses with their big guns. Their shells burned visible paths to targets.

We carried six 1,000-pounders which we dropped on an eight-inch coastal battery on Cap Camarat, despite the squadron record, which reported that we brought our bombs home. Before any of us wanted to relinquish his grandstand seat, hangers snapped and the bombs ticked out. Bay doors closed and our formation turned toward home. At the right-hand window in the radio room I tried for a final broad view of the event, but the moment had passed.

Back at Amendola we finished cleaning our guns shortly after noon, and almost immediately Flood and I caught a ride to our own beach, on the Adriatic. That afternoon in the warm sun, lying in languid detatchment, we tried to recall and absorb our experience of the morning. Our minds couldn't overcome the absurd constructions of time and geography.

Italy
Aug. 15, '44

Suppose you know we had a busy time today. All I can say is "We wuz there." It was a wonderful sight--and terrible too, as you can imagine. The funny thing about it was: tonite we all thought it was old stuff, and all of a sudden we heard "First news flashes" about it. ha! We even beat the reporters.

. . .Flood and I decided we should give our nerves a rest and caught a ride down to the beach. Boy what relaxation! We just sat in the surf and let the waves push us around. When we got tired of that, we layed in the sand and slept a while. We

are burned as red as tomatoes tonight.
Our work took us to where we visited
Napoleon's birthplace. It is nicer there than here.
Had trouble with our parleevoos, too. . .

B17 radio room, looking forward. Desk at left, door in center.

20. One Engine Out

We flew local slow-time tests for two planes on the 16th and 17th. These rarely lasted more than two and a half hours as pilots checked new engines under a variety of power settings. We often took along our watermelons and cans of beer to cool them off, and the flights gave the five who flew a chance to enjoy the view of the Adriatic Coast.

On one of these trips a friendly P51 pilot brought his plane in close over our right wing. Smiling and waving, he bounced his radiator housing a couple of times on our wing, almost as if we had three engines on that side. Then, without any signal, he pulled straight up and disappeared.

> *Italy*
> *August 16*

> *Still busy here, but doing OK. Very hot during the day and cool at night. . . Am getting pretty black in the sun. . .*

> *Italy*
> *August 17*

> *. . .Messed around here today and kept pretty busy. Got checked out on blinkers (Aldis lamp) this afternoon. . . Expect to be busy tomorrow*

--away from home. . .

On the 18th we went back to Ploesti--my fourth visit to Flak Alley in less than three weeks of combat flying.

August 18--Ploesti, Rumania. Americano- Romano oil refinery completely wiped out. 97th BG shows its stuff. Flak very intense and accurate. Saw oil fire and smoke thru my window and said over interphone: "Number two is on fire." Thought everybody knew about it--then Dale said, "Dammit, No. 2 engine is half gone--get ready to feather No. 2." Phil was using violent evasive action, but managed somehow to feather it before the fire got to the gas tanks. I had my flak vest off and my chute on and was standing in the bomb bay--ready to get out. Wolf, the bombardier, was calling out flak vollies to Phil. Made it back to base on three engines with less than 70 gals of gas left. 0800

Nothing clears the senses quite like an engine fire. Clumsy boots and other gear normally restricted our move- ments, but urgency creates its own speed and style. How- ever inelegantly, everybody in our crew acted as prescribed.

Engines caught fire on bomb runs most often be- cause flak had hit cylinders, sumps or oil lines. Pilots moved first to close that throttle down and feather that engine's propeller. Feathering meant pushing one of four red buttons on the instrument panel just forward of the throttle pedestal. That activated the pitch mechanism to turn propeller blades parallel to the line of flight. This feathering had to happen before the 37-gallon oil supply for that engine dropped too low to change pitch.

If a propeller failed to feather not only would it offer more wind resistance, but it would windmill and might "run away." This could turn the engine too fast, cause a screaming roar and finally vibrate so hard it could crystallize the prop shaft. Then the 500-pound propeller could fly off, further damaging the plane and its soft contents--the crew.

A prop could "run away" at any time if something damaged the constant speed governor mechanism or if its oil supply dropped too low. Under these conditions pilots trying to feather the prop usually set that throttle to idle in order to keep manifold pressure from building up. Super high pressure at high rpm could cause an engine to blow up.

Sometimes the 300 mph air stream blew out oil fires, allowing pilots to restart engines. In those cases crews had to watch cylinder head temperatures and oil pressure carefully because they never knew the extent of damage. If pilots desperately needed an engine's power and they knew it had been damaged anyway, they'd pour it on as long as the engine could help them.

Each engine carried a fire extinguisher which when activated forced a foamy mixture around the cylinders. The stuff usually wrecked the engines, and most pilots avoided using extinguishers if they thought the engine hadn't been damaged much or if they might want to restart it.

In this case our prop feathered and the oil fire died before it reached our main fuel tanks. When the black smoke stopped, I think I drowned out the sounds of war by yelling: "Fire's out!" The number two engine cowling and even some cylinders had disappeared. That engine couldn't help us any more, so Skok and Mabie had turned up the power in the other three.

Pilots always tried to stay with their formations, both for physical safety and the comfort of numbers, so increasing the power in three engines kept our B17 in formation. Our bomb run had been north to south, on a heading of 201 degrees at 27,400 feet, but the group by now had turned west for home, so power demands had dropped off.

Even if we had suffered damage to two engines and couldn't maintain our position, we might still have made it back. Throwing out guns, ammo and equipment would have helped in that case, and no crew valued even expensive gear more than their own skins. Also, by dropping the nose a degree or so, pilots often maintained their speed while falling below their parent formations. Group or squadron commanders in such instances tried to call friendly fighters in to add special protection for the straggler.

We lost one plane that day to flak. Eighteen of our planes reported damage, and ours was one of the two planes that reported major damage.

A concerned ground crew met us when we turned onto the hardstand that afternoon. They could see our stricken engine and the crew chief asked Skok immediately how much power he had been forced to use on the way home. He knew they'd spend all night replacing No. 2, but the other three had him worried. Skok assured him they had not been abused. Crew chiefs distrusted some pilots with their airplanes, but this crew chief and this pilot got along fine after the Aug. 18 mission.

Checking the oily, smoky remains, we concluded that a single chunk of 88 mm shell had ripped up our engine. Already a line officer had pulled up in a Jeep and literally taken an order for a new one and a cowling. Other ground crewmen had gone over the wing behind the engine, looking for holes in fuel tanks. Ground crews hated nothing so much as having to replace a plane's jelly/rubber self-sealing tanks. It meant removing whole wing panels.

Ground crews could change a B17's engines after 350 flying hours in combat areas. Some Cyclones lasted twice that long, however, depending on how hard they had been used. Good adjustment, new plugs and care helped, like regular dousing of intake filters. But avoiding long periods of flat-out power at 2,500 rpm had the biggest effect. Chiefs could tell when an engine needed replacing from the amount of oil emerging through its breathers.

Next time we flew her Maggie had a shiny aluminum cowling on her new No.2 engine.

Italy
August 18

> *. . . Had a very rough day today. Worst yet-- was really sweating blood for awhile. ha. You look at the papers for this date and find out the toughest target in Europe. . .*
> *When we were at chow tonight it started to pour. Our tent flaps were up, so our beds were soaked when we did get back.*

On the next day, Canadian and U.S. units met at Chambois, France, partially closing a trap on the German Seventh Army and parts of the Fifth Panzer Army.

We went after another Silesian synthetic oil plant on the 20th, this time an I.G. Farbenindustrie works a few miles east of Blechhammer in what had been Poland.

Briefing officers told us to be careful on our run at Oswiecim because we might confuse a nearby camp with the refinery. They said they didn't know the purpose of the camp. By the next spring we all knew. Oswiecim is the Polish spelling for Auschwitz.

August 20--Oswiecim, Poland. Synthetic oil plant 70 miles west of Krakow. Hit the target despite heavy flak barrage. 2nd Bomb Group drew most of it away from us--they made two runs and lost one ship. 0830

Everybody hated those "Three-sixties." A group leader, deciding the formation had made a poor bomb run, called off the drop and circled for another run at the same heading and altitude. By the second run flak gunners had the group's course and altitude well registered.

Italy
August 20

Another pretty busy day. The kind I like tho, because it wasn't as bad as some, and stacks up pretty well on my score.
Boy, you know? I haven't had a sick day in the Army yet. . . Kleiber has had a 12-day rest. I don't think he gets enough exercise. Looks too pale and weak. . .
Tonite, I cleaned up at the shower, changed my clothes, put on my good shoes, and tonite am relaxing. Have a book to read, so will be O.K. . . .
It has been trying to rain today, but hasn't succeeded as yet. Just wait a couple of months tho. .

*A day of leisure for us here. . . Read until
noon, and then caught a ride to the beach where we
swam and sunned all afternoon. . . intend to take it
easy the rest of the evening, as tomorrow will be
a busy day. . .*
*A Spitfire just buzzed us. I tho't he was
going thru our tent. ha.*

We enjoyed the ride to Lido di Siponto in an open
truck almost as much as swimming and sunning on the
beach. Flowering trees at the roadside perfumed the air and
carried us to a different, safer place. We'd take with us
whatever beer and Coke we could gather and cooled the
containers in a shallow creek that emptied into the Adriatic.

**August 22--Odertal, Germany. Oil and gas
refinery Knocked it out completely. 2nd Bomb
Group again draws the flak from us. Lots of flak,
but we are lucky again. 2nd lost another ship.
0810.**

This plant sat in the Oder Valley with Blechhammer's north and south plants. Mission planners found it hard
to bomb one target without getting flak from all of them.
During missions over this area the sky turned a distinct gray
from concentrated shell bursts.
Part of a letter to my brother:

Italy

August 22

Have been averaging every other day here, so are (sic) stacking them up in good order. Today was an "on" day and am I tired tonight. It was just average--got up at 4 a.m. and wasn't able to relax until about five tonight.

Part of a letter home:

Italy
August 22.

. . . Anyone who says it's an easy life is a fool. I'll take mine at home, and a lot easier. I heard a guy say that when he got home he was going to put a propeller on his shoulder and start walking. The first place where someone asked him what it was--well, that's where he was going to live.
The news is good. Sounds like it might not be too long now. No matter what the news is, we keep right on going. If it isn't over here before we finish our quota, we'll probably go east. . . .

Italy
Aug. 23

Just laying (sic) around today, but expect plenty of action tomorrow. Still very hot here. . . Boy, I'd like to see your flowers, Dad. From what you say, they must sure be pretty.

21. Fragged

August 24—Pardubice, Czechoslovakia.
Airfield—put it out of commission with
20-pound frags. One straggler was knocked
down when jumped by fighters. No flak to
speak of over the target. 0805.

According to our briefing for this mission the Russians had asked us to hit this airfield, a thorn in their side. Altogether, 600 heavy bombers went after transportation targets that day, mostly bridges in Hungary and Yugoslavia. We saw little flak, but spent an anxious few minutes over the target, nevertheless.

Our armorers loaded 20-pound fragmentation bombs about the size of an 88 mm shell, in clusters of six bombs each. A strapping device went around the bombs and hooked to a bomb release rack. After their release an arming wire parted the straps. Clusters opened somewhere below the plane and from that point each bomb fell independently, little propeller vanes turning to arm each nose fuse which was set to go off on contact.

Sounds great, but ours hung up, probably because of moisture freezing in the lower racks. The top racks, as scheduled, released their clusters, which fell on those hung up below. I yelled "Salvo!" and they went out--at least most of them. Bands around the clusters had opened, leaving several of our "daisy cutters" rolling ominously on the bomb bay catwalk.

Dolton saw them too, from the front. He told Wolf by interphone to keep the bay doors open. Each of us grabbed a walk-around oxygen bottle and got onto the catwalk. We figured that the little bombs hadn't armed themselves yet, but nudged at them gingerly anyway, pushing them off. Both of us felt relief when the bay doors finally closed.

We had to salvo our bombs on one other occasion when their hangers had frozen. On that trip the salvo switch dumped all but one 500-pounder which hung at the top of the left outside rack. Dolton, leaning over miles of open space, braced himself against the bomb itself as he triggered the hanger with a screwdriver. When the bomb dropped suddenly he had to jam his screwdriver through the skin of the plane to keep from falling.

After a month, all of us had adapted somewhat to being shot at. A surplus piece of flak jacket by now lay under the padding of my radio room seat. We had always considered ourselves more fortunate than infantrymen, but at least during a shelling the ground protected a foot soldier from fragments in 180 degrees.

Italy
August 24

. . . Today was another hard day. A long ride, but the scenery was beautiful. Could have kicked myself for forgetting my camera.

Sorry you can't get many cigarettes to sell. I wish I could send you my "rations" every week. Have stopped getting them now, because I have

Flood stocked up pretty well. . .

I had started smoking cigarets when I entered the Army. For a time after we arrived in Italy, however, the weekly ration turned out to be off-brands that tasted awful. In self-defense, several of us turned to pipes and cigars. Each man could get a can of 49 reasonably good cigars a week. For several months one could navigate at night through our bivouac area from pinpoints of glowing butts.

On the day after our Pardubice mission the German commander in Paris surrendered the city to French and American troops.

> *Italy*
> *August 25,*

> *. . . Had another busman's holiday today.*
> *Had to go pick up some officers coming back from*
> *rest camp. Didn't do any work tho--just watched the*
> *scenery go by. Got a good dinner out of it too. . .*
> *Don't you worry about me getting nervous.*
> *It's just that we are so tense for awhile. A little*
> *sleep and we are as good as new. . .*

On that day five of us flew a "jukin'" ship down to Crotone, near the sole of the Italian boot. Every group had at least one of these planes that had been taken out of combat because of serious battle damage. All turrets, armor and guns had been removed and we used the ships for general transport. Our orders said to pick up some officers at an old German fighter strip.

The extremely light plane flew like a kite. We found the dirt strip in about an hour and buzzed it to look it over. No buildings. A wrecked Westland Lysander sat with one wingtip on the ground near the tree line. The strip appeared short and trees surrounded it, but Skok and Mabie agreed that our lack of weight would help us. After a standard approach, Skok slipped the plane in close to the treetops at one end and had to brake hard before we reached the other end.

He cut the engines and a couple of us hopped out. Two full colonels walked toward us, wearing big grins. They both carried B-4 bags and turned to wave toward the trees. Three young women in summer nurse's uniforms came in sight, also carrying bags. We discussed with them for a minute where they might ride, and settled on the nose. The two colonels pulled themselves up through the nose hatch, but I took the nurses through the waist door and the length of the plane. They seemed embarrassed, but we tried to act as if we did this every day.

They wanted to go to Bari, so we rolled to the other end of the dirt strip and Skok spun the ship around as close to the trees as he could get. Holding the brakes as long as possible, he finally let go and we headed for the greenery at the other end. He held the plane on the ground until we ran out of strip, then seemed to jump the plane straight up.

We let our passengers out at Bari and somebody on the flight line invited us to lunch at a posh mess for transient crews. While we ate we learned that 15th Air Force brass often took nurses along for "rest and recreation" at a hunting lodge near the Crotone strip. Sort of a reward for superior work, we guessed, but carting them home in a four-engine plane seemed a bit much. All five had appeared a little pale when they left the plane. We hoped that by giving

them a close look at the trees during takeoff we had contributed to their queasiness.

*. . . Eddie Flood and I went swimming and
collected a little more tan. . . Bought 4 more
canteloupe tonite. . .*

*No--I don't think I want to write anything for
the paper--couldn't give them a satisfactory picture
of Italy. Will let some guy who hasn't seen anything
else do it. Have seen just about every country in
Europe from where you can see them. Italy is
certainly the most drab, dirty, and backward of
them all. The others are quite beautiful. . . Hope
to complete this world trip so I can appreciate a
wonderful place to live that is North Dakota. . .*

Italy
August 27

*Another day of rest--and will have one
tomorrow, too. Guess maybe they have forgotten
about us. ha. Well, it's OK--maybe I'll go to town
tomorrow. . . Glad you put the money in the bank
for me. . . It was pretty hot this afternoon and we
had a lot of blowing dust. The mosquitos are about
to eat us alive. I think I'll blow out this candle a
while before I go to bed so they will leave. . .*

Italy
August 29

162

. . . Not a busy day for us--so we laid around all morning, then Flood and I went swimming all P.M. That beach is a lifesaver for us.

I guess you know I didn't write yesterday. Went into town before noon intending to spend the day loafing. Met three or four of my old radiomen buddies who are in other outfits near here. We talked over old and new things, went to a movie in the afternoon, ate a lunch at the Red Cross, then went to a combined British and American service stage show. The name of it was "Hi Gang." --You wrote of listening to Bebe Daniels' program from England. Well, she was the star of that stage show. . . They had the famous "Esquires" (GI band), a dancing team, two Limey comedians. . . some very good entertainment. . .

Italy
August 30

We loafed around and read all morning, and then Eddie and I went swimming all afternoon. . . I think Bob had it worse on his maneuvers than we do here. . .

August ended for us as it had started: hot. Combat had been just as warm. The 15th Air Force lost 2,426 air crewmen during the month, 30 percent of its flying rosters. Replacements, as in July, arrived in squadrons almost daily, like tourists with all their baggage. Unpainted planes came to outnumber the older, camouflaged ships as those were lost.

163

The 97th had flown in the last mission against Ploesti on the 19th. Attacks on the refineries there had cost 350
bombers, more than at any other target. This figure included
45 British Halifaxes and Wellingtons. In addition to bombing refineries, the RAF at this time dropped 1,400 mines in
the Danube River at night. Their object was to try to halt
fuel shipments to Germany by barges, which carried 60 percent of Ploesti's oil. Our raids against oil would continue, of
course, but now mostly against synthetic refineries.

Co-pilot Dick Mabie adjusts the throttles.

22. The POW's Return

September 1–Tesica, Jugoslavia. Bombed a large and important railroad bridge. A bottleneck in the German supply line to the Russian front. Completely destroyed it. No opposition. 0500

Soviet armies threatened to cut off German units in all of the Balkans, so Jerry had started moving northwestward as early as the middle of August. To interdict the Germans we bombed bridges and airfields as far south as Greece.

Italy
Sept. 1

. . . Did an easy one today. Not even a day's work. Wish more of them were like that. Very hot today. . .

Approaching Soviet armies forced most German defenders to pull out of Ploesti and Bucharest during the last week in August. They left behind 1162 imprisoned allied air crewmen who had been downed at Ploesti and held in Bucharest. These prisoners now got their chance at freedom. Their Romanian wardens, wanting to gain some favor, started on Aug. 26 to move prisoners to barracks south of Bucharest.

The ranking prisoner, Lt. Col. James A. Gunn, and a Romanian air force captain, Constantine Cantacuzene, flew in an ME109 to San Giovani, Italy. They arranged with 15th Air Force brass in Bari to have U.S. planes pick up the POWs and bring them to Italy before Soviet forces arrived in Bucharest to complicate the process.

Buses transferred the prisoners to Popesti Airfield near Bucharest. On Aug. 31, 36 B17s from the 97th and 2nd Bomb Groups started shuttling between Popesti and Bari, each plane carrying 20 POWs. U.S. fighters covered each flight of 12 Seventeens. The operation, called "Reunion," continued through Sept. 3.

Nearly everybody in the 97th seemed to know about this rescue activity, but our crew didn't take part. That disappointed us, especially when on Sept. 2 we learned that Chuck Grayson had returned among the POWs. We had scarcely dared hope for his survival, but he appeared almost magically after spending nearly six weeks in enemy custody. He had allowed his beard to grow, and his previously short mustache now spanned at least five inches. He had lost weight but appeared hard and vigorous. I took several pictures. The Army planned to send him home, so he spent most of a day telling us his story as he sat on Skok's cot.

He told us that it all started on July 22, just after he had released his bombs over a Ploesti refinery. He said he had leaned forward to watch the bombs drop when everything suddenly became very noisy and windy. The plane's plexiglass nose had blown off and he said he knew he was falling. Wind whipped the hose of his oxygen mask around his face, so he ripped it away.

He had snapped his parachute to his harness before the bomb run, probably his best move of the day. Flak still burst around him and he was very high, so he decided to fall a while before pulling the ripcord. He said he had almost entered the smoke screen at the target when he yanked the D-ring. He remembered a terrible jerk and swinging once or twice before hitting the ground unexpectedly.

Charlie hadn't seen the ground and the landing caused him to bite his tongue. He said he got out of his harness and almost immediately ran into another American crewman, a co-pilot from a B24. The two joined in a desperate scramble for safety, their efforts accompanied by the sound of exploding bombs and the pounding of antiaircraft guns.

Some time later the two approached a stream in a search for water. Grayson needed to clean up his mouth because his tongue had swelled and become painful. At this point a farmer "captured" the two and turned them over to local military people.

About 40 percent of crewmen survived from planes shot down at Ploesti. Romanians held captured officers like Grayson in a large Bucharest schoolhouse, the Central Seminary for Women. Captured enlisted men wound up in a building at the Regina Elizabeth military hospital near the railroad yards. Men in neither group ate very well, or very much. Charlie said their guards served up a lot of watery cabbage soup and scraps of fish. Eyes from the fish heads often watched him from the bowl.

Now that he was back in Italy the Army gave Charlie some new clothes, orders to return home, a jump in rank to First Lieutenant, and a Purple Heart. The medal, awarded because of his injured tongue, would go in the bottom of his barracks bag, he said. He didn't want to have to explain how he got it.

Italy
Sept. 2

     Boy, we all feel pretty good tonite. Grayson walked into Skok's tent today--with a beard about an inch long. He looks darn good for having been a P.W. in the clink for nearly six weeks. . . He will probably be going home soon. Bet his wife will certainly be glad to see him. We're sweating out M. now.
     . . . Went into town today before we went swimming. We went to a place and ordered fried fish, fried spuds, and spaghetti. They threw in a bottle of white wine, too. The bill for the five of us was $9.00 but I guess it was worth it. . .
     The news is pretty good, isn't it? I always listen to the BBC news between weather reports. . .

Because it had been bombed heavily Foggia had no restaurants beyond what little we could get at the Red Cross Club. For our party to celebrate Charlie's return, we found a family of about eight who would fix us meals--as long as we gave them our order, and money, in advance. This Italian family scrounged the black market for food and, of course, ate it with us. Though oily, "Mama's" cooking filled the bill. I imagine this informal kind of food business helped several families through some rough times.

We didn't know it yet, but our "good news" of the previous two weeks ran into a snag. After the breakout from Normandy, our troops had raced almost freely across

168

France. By the first week of September, however, they had outrun their supplies of food, ammunition and gasoline. Their pause gave the Germans time to regroup, and killed our hopes for a rapid end to the war.

September 4--Genoa, Italy. Bombed 7 large German subs in harbor for repairs. Sunk 4 and damaged others and demolished repair sheds. Very intense and accurate flak, but were lucky-- getting out with about a dozen holes. 0730.

Italy
Sept. 4, 1944

. . . Had a pretty rough time today. Sure sweat, but made out O.K. Dad, when those reporters say "no opposition"--they just "wasn't there" that's all. We don't get that ventillation "built in.". . .

Will be glad when I can listen to WNAX instead of "dirty gurty (sic) from Berlin." They do give us some pretty good music tho. . .

Yesterday afternoon we had a duststorm that makes those N.D. howlers look pretty tame. We had to put on our gas masks. The next thing we knew it was a drenching rain. Everything that we had that was full of dust turned to mud. We are still trying to get things clean. . .

Phil and Dick went to Rest Camp at Capri. From there they will go to Rome. The rest of us will be up for it soon.

. . . Just made my Staff rocker (fourth stripe). . .

Italy's weather had undergone its usual fall transformation. Showers had drenched us occasionally in July and August, but matters changed drastically with this storm. We pulled down our tent walls that until now had flown horizontally to allow the air to pass through.

Our tent suddenly grew too cramped, and dark. Next day we extended the canvas again and made vertical walls from plywood cases. These light containers had held streamlined metal drop tanks for P38s, and some prescient people in supply had squirreled them away. We cut shorter pieces to fill in the tent corners, to which we added small windows, cut from plexiglass scrounged from the boneyard.

The tent, having started life at Tafaraoui in Morocco, leaked nearly everywhere. We couldn't get a new one, so we painted it with a mixture of tar and oil. It smelled terrible for a couple of weeks, and we must have added a hundred pounds to its weight, but it shed water.

Operations folks didn't schedule us to fly for nine days because of the absence of our pilots. We could have volunteered for "bastard" crew assignments, but somehow nobody had told us. Bad things seemed to happen to us when we flew with other crews, so maybe our ignorance paid off.

Italy
Sept. 5, 1944

This afternoon Charlie, Ed, Tuk and I went to the beach and browsed around. It's sure swell, splashing in the surf. Charlie looks as good as ever. Tough constitution, I guess.
. . . There are all kinds of rumors flying

*around here now. I hope they are true. The news
seems to be pretty good.*

*Autumn is in the air around here. The nights
are getting a lot colder and the mosquitos are really
fierce. More wind than before, too. . .*

Nearly everyone in our squadron at this time spent
his nights scrounging the countryside for material things that
would help prepare him for a cold, wet winter. We used
squadron vehicles and went after British and American military bivouacs. Few got caught because any soldier or truck
looked like all the rest. We left the Italians alone, mostly because they didn't own much that we wanted. Our midnight
requisitioning often resulted in whole truckloads of lumber
and crushed rock. We even picked up some new tents one
night at the 2nd Bomb Group.

Radio operator's view through bomb bay. Catwalk at right.

23. Unpolished Heroes

Italy
Sept. 6

> *Well, it happened. The 97th finally got the*
> *Presidential Citation they've been expecting. Had*
> *a big ceremony today. Even had the General down*
> *here. . .*
> *Did you get the pictures? I hope they got*
> *thru O.K. Am sending one I took of Skok by our*
> *tent. He really looks like the old "flip" in this one.*
> *We all kid him about his "moustacho" that he's*
> *trying to grow.*

We had learned of the Unit Citation about a week
earlier. The 97th's actions at Steyr, Austria, on Feb. 24 had
caught somebody's attention. Our notice said Gen. Nathan
Twining, 15th Air Force commander, would present the
award. The notice said all four squadrons would stand in
formal dress review.

Formal dress review, indeed. In planning this affair
nobody had allowed for uniforms. Few people in any
squadrons owned a complete summer kit, especially those
ground crewmen who had been overseas for a couple of
years. Many hadn't even stood at attention for a year or
more, let alone march in review. No matter. A couple of Ita-

lian carpenters soon built a low wooden platform in the wheat stubble just north of group headquarters.

The day of reckoning arrived. To avoid forming first and marching to the "parade grounds," we walked there, leisurely. The skies threatened rain but somebody gathered us into four more-or-less cohesive mobs and called us to as much attention as we could manage. Many wore no head covering. Most had cut their GI shoes into sandals. Pants and shirts matched only by chance.

Twining and some of his aides rode up in an olive drab staff car. In a few minutes he had read the citation into a P.A. system microphone. He ended by saying that this was the "finest looking group of fighting men" he had ever seen.

Somebody started a recording of "Stars and Stripes Forever." An officer yelled, "Pass in review!" Four amoeba-like formations shuffled in an arc past the wooden stand. Individual soldiers talked to other soldiers or oggled the brass. Dust from the stubble field soon covered both the soldiers and the dignitaries.

Part of a letter to my brother:

> *Italy*
> *Sept. 8, 1944*

> *. . . Congrats on the zebra arm you're getting, fella. Guess they appreciate a good msg. handler--. . . I'm still going batty listening to static and Axis Sally. Had my receiver smashed by flak once, but the darned thing worked and that meant I had to listen to it all the way back. . .*

> *Did I tell you that I got the Air Medal? Guess we can go into the scrap metal business after the war. . .*

I had not adopted quite so casual an attitude about the war. My words, like those of many 19-year-olds, reflected both a pride and impatience with day-to-day wartime activity, especially when writing to an older brother. Air Medals and their Oak Leaf Clusters came to air crewmen after an arbitrary number of missions. Nobody knew the number, which varied in my case between six and 14.

Part of a letter home:

Italy
Sept. 8, 1944

Happy birthday, Dad. . .

We are about 100 yards from chow and we make it in about 10 seconds. . . We have a little dispensary here that does all our minor medical attention, and the big hospitals are in Foggia.

Our job will be rough right up to the end here, and when this is thru, we may have to fight Japs. These A.P. writers who say the "worst is over," and "no opposition," etc., are guys who sit behind desks, waiting for us to radio results.

Hey you guys, this mail service isn't good enough for you to start worrying whenever you don't hear from me for a couple of days. Yesterday, for instance, I didn't write because I went to town with Kleiber. Yes, he's O.K. They just grounded him because he was short of red corpuscles. He's flying as usual. . .

Italy
Sept. 9

*. . . We have a little one burner gas stove
and we have a lb. of coffee, so are going to brew up
a gallon or two tonite.*

*Italy
Sept. 10
Sun. P.M.*

*. . . The Red Cross had a blowout in town
today. . . They had a little carnival, G.I. orch.,
coffee and do-nuts, etc. . . .*

*It's getting colder every nite. . . I use two
blankets over me now in bed to keep warm. I hope
we don't stay here thru the cold, wet winter. . .*

*You may get about 4 letters at once from me.
Will wait till Flip and Dick come back and have
them censor them all at once. I gave them my
camera to use in Rome. Hope they get some good
pics. . .*

*Flood and I have decided to put in for rest
camp one of these days. We feel swell, but may as
well enjoy ourselves a little. . .*

Skok and Mabie took three rolls of film in Rome but
all of it was lost, including several pictures I had taken of
Grayson during his short stay with us. For processing, I
gave the rolls to a friend at group S2 who had developed
film for me before. I went over to his darkroom to pick up
our pictures and learned that he had been sent home. Nobody could find our film.

Italy

Sept. 11, '44
Mon. A.M.

. . . Well, weather held us back this morning. Sure glad we didn't go as it was a "ruff and tuff" joint to go looking for trouble. Milburn had his tough luck up there. Hope he's O.K.

I guess it's O.K. to give you the number of missions. I've 21 now, and 29 to go. They say you are only half thru when you've finished 49 as you really sweat blood on the last. . .

Weather from this point on frustrated us on many days. We lost a lot of sleep and went through our usual pre-mission labors only to get a red light from the tower at about 6:30 a.m. Then we'd have to pack our gear back to the shack and catch a ride to group. At least we didn't have to clean our guns.

Italy
Sept. 12

. . . One of the radiomen was grazed in the leg by a big chunk of 88 mm today. Just sliced his heated suit. I hope those Japs aren't as good at shooting as these Krauts. . .

The G.I. laundry has quit now, so we will have to take our stuff over to a farmhouse to get washed. . .

Will be pretty busy tomorrow. I hope I get a lot of missions in here in Italy. It's better to be stationed here than a lot of other places. Even the war news from the Pacific sounds good tonite. . .

A letter home shouldn't have included such gore, even though we saw crewmen wounded on nearly every mission. Capt. Luke Remley, our squadron flight surgeon, spent many days at the hospital in Foggia working on our wounded. He operated for hours one afternoon to save the legs of a tail gunner. Flak had shattered both knees.

Every crew at one time or another had to treat wounded men on the way back to base. Someone on each crew, usually the co-pilot, took charge of emergency treatment. Each plane carried two or three first aid packets which held scissors, bandages, sulfa powder and tiny doses of morphine, complete with needles.

As one might expect, uncontrolled bleeding from a wound caused most problems and concern. Also, part of the care involved keeping a wounded crewman warm. Trouble was, to get at a wound often meant cutting up a heated suit, thereby cutting off the warmth. In some cases, however, our extreme cold conditions helped stop severe bleeding. Everybody heard the story about a crewman whose wound in the buttocks wouldn't stop bleeding. His buddies finally knocked a hole in a plexiglass window and held his backside to the elements for instant frostbite.

The farm family where we took our laundry, only about half a mile away, turned out to be dependable cleaners. Each washing, which we had done only about once every two weeks, cost a package of cigarets. We had no bedsheets, so the payment was about right.

Around this time a delegation from the U.S. Congress toured our squadron area in a personnel carrier. The visitors included a woman. As they drove in from the highway they passed our latrine, a screen-enclosed affair which stood about 20 feet from the entrance road. One of the guys in the johnny at the time said the congresswoman had a first-hand look at our country's defenses.

September 13—Blechammer (sic), Germany. Aviation gas plant. We hit the wrong target—a refinery just 4 miles So. of the one we were briefed on. Destroyed it, although the flak was as intense and accurate as Ploesti flak. We lost 7 ships—3 at once when a ship dropped its bombs on one below. The ship exploded, tearing a wing off one ship and the entire tail off another. 21 men got out of the three ships. Most of the ships came home on 3 engines. One landed on the island of Vis, in control of the Partisans, with only one engine going. (We pick up the crew at Bari two days later.) 0755.

Blechhammer had two synthetic refineries, so we didn't waste anything by hitting the wrong one. We learned later that we had lost five planes in the blasts. Crews in two other damaged ships finally returned. Losing a fourth of our planes in one mission, however, reminded us of how lucky we had been for a while. It didn't set well with anybody if we had, indeed, bombed our own planes. Even our intelligence people couldn't agree on what happened. Four of the planes lost were from 340th Squadron, which had formed Able Box. Our squadron had flown Charlie position. Some theorized that a straggler had dropped its load on planes below it. Others insisted that direct flak hits, not bombs, had caused the explosions. One person was killed, three were wounded and 51 were missing in action. It was the biggest loss for the group in any of its combat missions.

That afternoon on the way home we saw several B24s ditched in the Adriatic, apparently out of gas. That many ditchings usually meant that a group had been diverted to one or more secondary targets and perhaps had encountered strong headwinds. One of the ditched planes had slid up on the beach on the north side of the Gargano spur. Our air-sea rescue boats based along the Adriatic coast claimed to have rescued every air crew that hit the water that fall.

Italy
Sept. 13, 1944
6:30 P.M.

A hard day indeed. Nope, I can't agree that the worst ones are over.
Got up at 4 A.M. and have just now been able to sit myself down and relax. Have nothing to do tomorrow but a practice run, so should get rested up. . .
Saw five different European countries today, and didn't appreciate any of them. . .
There's a P38 buzzing us tonite. The joker must think the war is over. If he gets much closer, it will be, for him. . .

Fighter pilots based near us showed off regularly. We'd often get beat up by individuals who had completed their tours of duty. One P51 pilot spent about an hour on us one evening. He put his gear down and rolled his wheels on hard-packed ground between the squadron HQ buildings and our mess shack. Another, one of the red tails, buzzed

179

our tower repeatedly. Invited by radio to land, he replied: "No, thanks. I may be dumb, but I'm not that dumb."

Italy
Sept. 14

> *. . . Practice hop for two hours this A.M. . . .*
> *Took a can of grapefruit juice up with me and it was*
> *ice cold when we came down. . . A fellow who came*
> *back from a P.W. camp at Bucharest left a lot of*
> *canned stuff with us that he had gotten from home. .*

The colonel had called us out for practice at bomb-run formation flying. A good idea in view of our record the day before.

On that day the allied Combined Chiefs of Staff met in Quebec for the Octagon Conference, dealing mostly with the Far East.

Italy
Sept. 15

> *Got myself a good dinner today. We were*
> *ferrying another crew back home and stopped off*
> *for chow. May be busy tomorrow. . .*
> *We had a little shower this afternoon. Was*
> *so misty when we came back in the ship that we*
> *looked around for about ten min. before we could*
> *find the place. . .*
> *Had fresh fried eggs for breakfast this*
> *morning. . .*

Operations sent us down to Bari on that day to pick up the crew that had landed on the island of Vis on Sept. 13. A boat had brought them in. They told us they had landed on a very short strip and with only one engine turning over.

We cheered the cook and his fresh eggs. This sergeant had been a bartender before the war. He spent hours every day scouting for fresh food to relieve the tedium of canned meat and vegetables. Nobody appreciated him more than I.

Italy
Sept. 16

False alarm today. Was glad of it tho, as it gave us a chance to clean up the tent and sleep a lot. Will probably work tomorrow. . .

Getting colder every night here. Pretty cold getting up in the morning. Will have to get some kind of stove in here soon.

Have been bothered by mice here in the tent lately because of the fruit and stuff.

Squadron supply arranged a deal with some welders on the field to make a barrel stove for every tent. We had to take our turn, however. Meanwhile, I brought my unused insulated flying suit from the crew's shack and started sleeping in it.

Our youthful ingenuity solved the mouse problem. They ran around on the horizontal edges of our tent at night, so we dipped one tent corner about six inches and covered it with aluminum. We grooved the metal and directed it to a barrel half-filled with water. Our mice couldn't brake fast enough to save themselves from drowning. In a couple of days their ditchings had wiped them out.

September 17—Budapest, Hungary. We hit main marshalling yards in this big city. Flak was heavy and fairly accurate. No fighters reported. 0700.

Italy
Sept. 17, 1944

Another hard grind behind me tonite. I see on the bulletin board that I can rest tomorrow. The way I feel tonite, I think I can use some sleep. . .
Phil just made 1st Lieut. today. He's sure earned it. Hope he makes a pair of railroad tracks (Captain) before we leave. . .

That was the day the allies dropped three airborne divisions to try to capture Lower Rhine bridges and spearhead a ground operation toward the north. In Italy parts of the 85th Division took Mt. Altuzzo, breaking the back of the Germans' Gothic Line.

Italy
Sept. 18, '44

Looks like another holiday tomorrow. Sure hate to lay (sic) around. Wish we would have another spurt like we did at first. . .
In this week's Yank magazine a 15th A.F. G.I. gets back at some disrespectful remarks made by some 8th A.F. boys about our "easy" work.

Would like to take some of them along on some of those "easy" ones. Do you see the "Yank" there at home? It's pretty good. Shows the G.I.'s point of view like Ernie Pyle does. . .

Italy
Sept. 19, 1944

. . .Flood and I went to Foggia in the afternoon and stayed late for a show. . . Took some pictures of ruins, etc., there. There's not much to a picture tho, if you can't smell it. You should see how these people live in towns--and on the farms too. . .

The author during a visit to Foggia.

24. Wrecked by Flak

September 21—Debreczen, Hungary. Marshalling yards. We hit the target even tho the flak was unbelievably accurate & intense. They had our altitude perfectly. No fighters reported. 0800.

Twenty six planes in our group were damaged that day and we credited Jerry's accuracy at Debreczen to a couple of JU88s that sat out of range to one side during our bomb run, acting as flak spotters. They pulled off finally when streams of our 50 cal. tracers dropped near them.

At one time that fall someone at headquarters in Bari ordered tracers removed from our ammo. The order argued that each tracer round, inserted in a belt after every five rounds of API (armor-piercing incendiary), went wild and without effect.

We knew that tracers didn't fly straight. We raised the plea through our armament sections, however, that they more than compensated by letting Jerry know that we had seen him and had started firing. Nothing discouraged a German fighter pilot so much as seeing those white balls sailing past. In our minds, a deterred enemy at least equaled a dead enemy. Nearly all of our gunnery involved German planes barely within range--or out of range. Our indignant protests must have won the day, because nothing came of the order.

We had finished interrogation that day and out on the hardstand had started cleaning the ship's guns when we saw the straggler circling. The pilot appeared to have trouble lining up with the runway, making wide swings and firing distress flares. As we watched, he brought the plane in on the dirt strip of our runway.

I think we all yelled and pointed as the plane passed near our hardstand during its landing. We could see through a six-foot hole in the waist, torn horizontally across both gun positions. Only the floor and the vertical stabilizer at the top held front and rear parts of the plane together. Its tail wheel collapsed on the runway, causing the few remaining stringers in the top of the waist to buckle, and leaving the plane's middle to ride on the ball turret as it rolled to a stop.

We all jumped into Jeeps and trucks to get a closer look at the wreck. The plane, from the 429th Squadron of the 2nd Bomb Group, had been to Debreczen too. The burst had killed both waist gunners and the radioman. As we watched, somebody opened the ball turret from the outside. A gray-faced gunner staggered to his feet and leaned wobbily against the fuselage.

Finally able to speak, the ball-gunner said the blast had damaged his turret mechanism, oxygen lines and interphone. He found that he couldn't get out of his position and, even worse, couldn't talk to anybody. The landing had nearly driven him over the edge.

The front of this B17 showed no damage, but its pilots had lost all elevator and rudder control. Using aileron movement alone they adjusted their altitude and maneuvered in wide turns. Back in the States in 1945 several magazines ran pictures of this shattered plane, some in advertisements by Boeing.

Italy
Sept. 21

*Am pretty tired tonite. . . Kind of nervous
after a rough day. Maybe I should ask to be sent
to rest camp now instead of later on. Hate to do
it while I'm getting things done tho. . .*

*We are going to start wearing O.D.s (wool
olive drab) the first of Oct. Expect we will need
them too, as it is getting much colder.*

*Italy
Sept. 22.
6 P.M.*

*. . . Looks like we will earn our salt
tomorrow again. . . If anybody says "fight"
to me when this is over, I'll run off someplace
and go to sleep. Anything where it's peaceful. Have
lost too many friends. . .*

**September 23—Wels, Austria, marshalling yards
(5th alternate). We flew thru intense flak at
Brux, Czechoslovakia, where the oil refinery
was supposed to be our target. Target was
covered with clouds. We flew over the Skoda
Works at Pilsen, but it was also covered. We hit
marshalling yards at Wels, Austria. Several
ships had to land up the coast for fuel coming
back. We were in the air for 0850 hours and
bombed from 30,000 ft. No fighters reported.
Temp. was 43 F below zero. Flood lost his
oxygen mask. We decided on giving him my**

mask and for me to breathe out of the oxygen
hose. Nearly froze my face and hands. 0850.

We appreciated our pilots, who knew how to lean
out fuel mixtures on these long trips where we flew over
several targets. Those crews who didn't take care of fuel
consumption landed all the way from Rimini to Pescara.
They begged gasoline at RAF fighter bases and returned to
Amendola the next day.

None of us in our crew wanted to turn back when
Flood discovered that he lacked an oxygen mask. Nobody
could watch him way back in the tail, but the waist gunners
could keep an eye on me through the bulkhead door, so he
used my mask. I sucked my oxygen directly from the hose,
using a nylon glove between my lips and the metal coupling.

Our faces normally frosted over around our masks,
but sucking from the hose for five hours built a mound of
rime on my face and over my left hand. I managed to log
messages, but didn't even try manning the gun. My face
usually chapped around the outline of my mask, but all of it
was red and sore for a week after this mission.

Increased cloud cover over European targets forced
us in September to rely increasingly on Mickey, or P.F.F.
bombing. Officially called H2X, this British-developed system bounced radar signals off the ground. It displayed a
very rough picture of buildings and other ground features
on a cathode-ray tube in the plane.

By this time, on just about every mission, a Mickey-
equipped B17 led the group. Instead of a ball turret it carried in that position a white dome which contained a para-
bolic radar antenna. A Mickey operator sat at a desk on the
right side of the radio room, adjusting knobs and staring
into a masked screen. He referred to maps made earlier

from radar returns of the route and the target to help him locate and line up on the objective. Operators usually had trouble identifying targets and required a long approach to get us set on the bomb line.

We would have given up trying to bomb in Europe on many days without Mickey, but the device didn't come near the Norden bomb sight in accuracy. During the final four months of 1944, 70 percent of 15th Air Force missions and 80 percent of 8th Air Force missions resorted to radar bombing. Post-war estimates placed the average amount of error that winter at about two miles.

That's why we always tried for visual drops, even if we had to fly to several alternate targets. P38 weather planes flew high over all our briefed targets that fall, checking cloud cover as we approached. We'd divert to an alternate objective, or even to a third, if our weather pilots advised it.

The Norden sight allowed us good target patterns even from 30,000 feet or more. The sight involved optics, calculators and gyroscopes, and the bombardier used an air speed indicator and altimeter to help set up the sight, which also accounted for ground speed, ballistics of bombs, trail and drift. Once adjusted for a target, it automatically set up the correct spot on the bomb run to release the bombs.

The bombardier could set the order, number and interval of bomb release. He controlled the airplane on the bomb run, usually with the sight connected to the Honeywell autopilot, but he could use the pilot's direction indicator (PDI). If he chose to use the autopilot, adjustments to the bombsight also adjusted the plane's lateral controls. With the PDI method, adjustments to the bombsight were transmitted to a visual display instrument in the cockpit, telling the pilot which direction to turn.

At the IP, the beginning of the bomb run, the pilot trimmed the plane for precise altitude and airspeed. He maintained this straight-and-level flight for the entire run and avoided any skidding or slipping. Poor alignment on bomb runs had caused a lot of inaccurate bombing back in 1942.

Actually, in group formation bombing, all the bombardiers dropped their bombs at the moment the lead bombardier released his. Briefings prescribed alternate lead bombardiers, and all bombardiers normally set up their sights, prepared to act on their own if necessary.

We kidded bombardiers a lot for adding their body weight to our load. Toward the end of the war the 8th Air Force replaced some officer/bombardiers with enlisted "toggliers." Most crews in the 15th kept their bomb droppers but added other responsibilities. Bombardiers made oxygen checks by interphone every 1,000 feet and ordered test-firing of guns. Bombardiers also helped navigators locate check points along the course and helped point out flak vollies for pilots.

At the end of the war the Army Air Forces estimated that 75 percent of their bombs fell within 1,000 feet of the aiming point. Few bombardiers or air crewmen believed that figure.

Our bombs, nearly always three tons to a plane, ranged from little 20-pound "daisy cutters" to 2,000-pounders, filled with an explosive called RDX, which was a mixture of TNT and cyclonite. To add to German consternation at the target some bombs carried fuses delayed from one to 144 hours.

The Fifteenth Air Force tried a new radio-guided bomb tail device called Azon on 1,000-pound bombs on April 24 and 29, and May 13, 1944. A bombardier, using an

Azon transmitter in a specially equipped B17, could steer a bomb laterally to a target. Azon bombs had some success but were limited, both in numbers and because they couldn't be steered longitudinally.

Italy
Sept. 23

I never want to spend another day like this one. Am sure tired tonite. Have the day off tomorrow so can get rested up again. . .
I think this altitude is affecting me a little. My kidneys aren't acting natural. All of us are troubled the same way. It may be that it's caused by riding in the trucks so much. . .

We looked everywhere for the source of our kidney pains. We finally consulted Doc Remley, who asked us a few questions then invariably told each of us, "Ace, you aren't drinking enough water." We had not filled up with much fluid at breakfasts before missions, trying to avoid using the relief tube in the bomb bay, especially after we had dressed and had plugged into oxygen.

The doc suggested that we drink more and use the tube in the plane just before we plugged into oxygen and again just after we unplugged on the way home. We followed his advice which, as usual, took care of our problem. He admitted, though, that it was easy to give such counsel, never having had to seek relief at 40 below zero and encased in long johns, heated suit, coveralls, Mae West and harness.

Air crewmen broke new ground every day in ingenious adaptations. If one could avoid creating a flame, for example, smoking in a plane, even around oxygen, created little danger. Those who had to smoke tried to use a flameless punk lighter. One bombardier insisted on cigars and used an old-style oxygen mask that had two sponge-filled exhaust holes near his mouth. He removed one of the sponges and poked a cigar into his mouth through the hole.

Oxygen masks had their effects too. They usually thwarted would-be beard-growers, but Wolf, our bombardier, accommodated both. He ignored our derisive words about the grotesque shape his beard assumed after every mission.

Italy
Sept. 24

Went to a blinker (Aldis signal) class this A.M. Got a shot for typhus this afternoon. . .
We have a 165-gal. droppable belly gas tank now that we are going to rig up in the tree for our water supply. The water truck will fill it up when it gets empty. We get tired of carrying our water whenever we want to wash up. . .

We hoisted the belly tank into our almond tree, then ran a line into our tent. Turning a small valve now gave us water for our wash basins. We usually washed and shaved in our tents and used cold water or heated it on a small gas burner until we received our tent heater.

Italy
Sept. 25

It rained all morning and we all read to pass

the time.

Italy
Sept. 26

Boy--I don't think I'm going to like this
weather. It was really cold all day. . .
Ed and I went to town to the show in the
afternoon. The shows (movies) aren't bad here.
Sound isn't so hot. . . have to wait between reels
while the reels are changed. . .
We do all our private frying in olive oil.
It gives it a very good flavor I think. . . You asked
me why we didn't buy milk. They tell us the cattle
around here have a high disease rate, so that dairy
stuff isn't safe. . .

Italy
Sept. 29

. . .Well, the rains came--and are to come
again and again. All of this powdery dust which
is Italy has turned into a sea of mud--which is Italy
--and ankle deep too, with indications of getting
deeper.

Italy
Sept. 30

Another wet and dismal day. Doesn't seem
to be able to stop raining. In a tent a person sure
notices it, too. Everything seems damp and you can
hear the water running down the roof. . .

192

I was on a practice hop this afternoon, but
we were forced right back down in a rainstorm.
Sure murky...
We were paid this afternoon. I got $145.55.
... The mud is getting thicker all the time.
We will get overshoes when it gets too deep for our
shoes...

September had brought changes, but mostly in the weather. From now on the weather in Italy ordered our lives.

Skok (left), Dolton, Mabie and Flood wait for green light before a mission.

2nd Bomb Group plane that landed at Amendola on Sept. 21, 1944.

Above, B17
flight deck.

Right, waist
looking forward.

25. Gray Skies, Brown Mud

Italy
Oct. 1

. . . The place is a sea of mud and water. We've dug more ditches today, trying to drain most of the water away from our tent. It's a major project going to and from chow as it's so slippery and easy to slide into the mud holes and slit trenches they have scattered around the area. . .

Read about the long hunting season you are to have. . . Hope you have another open winter so there will be some for me to shoot. Am tired of shooting at birds that shoot back. . .

Italy
Oct. 3

Another cold damp day. It's keeping us on the ground, and it looks like we'll be here forever. Haven't got a stove yet, so we spend the time in the sack or with a heavy coat on.

I guess you know I made Tech. the first of the month. . .

. . . You couldn't find Capri on the map? It's just off Naples harbor. I'd rather go to Rome to rest

camp now that it's cold. It was mostly swimming
and boating at Capri, they said. . .

I've just 27 missions in now.

Italy
Oct. 4, '44

Spent most of my time reading "How Green
Was My Valley" today. . . The rest were busy tho. I
will be tomorrow. The weather has changed. . .
Our tent is a mess. Seems like we just exist to eat
and sleep. . .

I went over to supply today and drew an
overcoat and two more pair of woolen underwear. .

Dick (Mabie) went to rest camp again. Can't
see how he expects to finish up. . . .

My weather forecast for the next day erred. We took
off and headed north, but in about an hour were called back
because of bad weather moving into Italy. By now, although
we usually flew with our own crew, we had all volunteered
to fly in bastard crews. These were made up of men who
wanted to finish their missions as soon as possible and those
who were "left over" when most of their own crews had
completed their missions or were casualties. Sometimes we
simply filled in for casualties, for those on rest leave and for
men who had completed their tours. On some missions no
two of us came from the same crew. We didn't especially
like such assignments, but they helped us to reach the magic
numbers.

Italy
Oct. 6

The weather was bad both yesterday and today. . .

Lasota came over to see me at about 4 P.M. yesterday and we decided to go to town for some do-nuts and coffee. . . We had seen the show at the Flagella Theatre so we didn't stay. . .

You're sure lucky you haven't this kind of gumbo there. It's the stickiest stuff I've ever seen. . .

The sound of rattling mess kits signaled our chow time as air and ground crewmen slipped and slid among dripping trees and tents on their way to eat. Those who couldn't maintain their footing in the muck went down in a great metallic clatter. Those fortunate enough to remain erect cheered loudly at the style in which a fallen comrade struggled to regain his feet. Falling in the mud usually called for a retreat to the shower tent--and a change to dry clothes.

October 7,--Vienna, Austria. Lobau oil and gas refinery 4 mi. south of city. Destroyed target. Observed large oil fires. Very intense flak, but not too accurate as our altitude was 29,000 feet. Only 4 holes. Saw one enemy fighter go down in flames. No losses. 0735.

Part of a letter to my brother:

Italy
Oct. 7,
9 p.m.

. . . Had a long, hard, rough one today. . .
we were pretty lucky again and fortunate in having
the kind of ships that can get us up good and high.
Sure pity the B24 boys. . .

This place is just one big quagmire. Ankle-
deep mud that sticks like gum--everywhere. . . Every
once in a while we go to town. . . to see Papa Henri
and have him fry us some eggs and potatoes. It's a
nice private home we ran across by accident. . .

> *Italy*
> *Oct. 8,*
> *9 p.m.*

A wet day--which limited operations to the
sack and a good book. . . Just got out of the tent
to eat. . .

> *Italy*
> *Oct. 9, '44*
> *5 P.M.*

Another rainy day. . .
We do get to go home when we've finished
50 missions. That's the whole idea of finishing up
quick. . .

**October 10,--Mestre, Italy. Marshalling yard in
the port city of Venice, Italy. Hit the target on
the nose. Flak was moderate, but concentrated
and accurate. Flood gets hit on his flak helmet.
0550.**

Italy
Oct. 10, '44

Pulled the curtain down on No. 30 today. . .
It was another of those "milk runs" that often turn
out so differently. Flood has a knot on his head
tonite. Those good old helmets. . .

Our mission planners usually plotted bomb run headings to take advantage of prevailing or expected winds over
the target. For this one our group caught a significant boost
in speed at our altitude. The navigator said our ground
speed was right at 320 mph.

October 11--Vienna, Austria. 20th birthday.
Briefed on So Ordinance (sic) depot, but clouds
entirely covered target and could not pick it up
with Mickey. Brought bombs home. 0650.

We didn't quite bring them home. Because so many
of our bombs contained delaying fuses we dropped these in
a prescribed area in the middle of the Adriatic. Presumably,
they killed fish there for a couple of days.

Italy
Oct. 11,

Another long hard day--with no action or
results. Just a long period of sweating it out. A
heck of a way to celebrate my 20th birthday. . .
. . .Tuck had another close call with his
oxygen yesterday. I wish they would ground him
and send him home now before something worse

happens. He just isn't able to do what he's supposed to.

Tuk Kleiber had awful oxygen habits and we had to watch him. He'd get out of his ball turret and get on a walk-around oxygen bottle so he could relieve himself. When he returned to his turret he'd sometimes dispose of the little oxygen bottle then hook up his heat and his interphone lines before plugging his mask into his oxygen hose in the turret. Lack of oxygen doesn't provide many warnings. He'd simply pass out.

On this day Russ Grove noticed him sitting motionless in the turret and yanked him out. Russ then gave him a shove forward into the radio room. I plugged him into the extra oxygen outlet there and flipped the emergency switch to 100 percent. His color soon changed from gray to pink, but his eyes remained closed and he didn't stir as we crossed the target. We kidded Tuk for weeks as the world's only crewman who ever slept through the flak on a bomb run.

Skok recommended and got a Distinguished Flying Cross for Grove because he pulled Tuk from the turret. Its construction made the ball the most protected position in the plane, but wouldn't protect a gunner from himself. I had my own doubts about the position. The ball gunner couldn't wear his parachute pack while he was in it.

October 14,–Blechhammer, Germany. North aviation gas plant. We make two runs and finally drop them squarely in the central area. Although we go in at 31,000' the flak was still intense and very accurate. 42 F below zero, but we were warm enough. In air nearly 10 hours. Sweated out gas coming home. Engines kept cutting out

and one died just above the strip. Had about 12 gallons when we parked.

When a main gas tank went dry the engine it was feeding quit, unless one transferred fuel from another tank. Electric pumps operated by switches in the bomb bay transferred the gasoline, but any transfers had to cross the center of the plane. Therefore, to move gas from one tank on the left side to another tank on the left side, one had to move it first to a tank on the right side, then pump it back across to the left.

On our return to base from this mission Dolton sat in the bay bulkhead door at the rear of the flight deck, throwing switches at Mabie's direction, trying to keep a little fuel in each main tank. After we parked our ground crew drained the tanks to look for holes. They gathered only 12 gallons, not enough even to warm up the engines. The group lost a plane on the mission.

Italy
Oct. 14

. . . Got up at 3:30 this morning and just finished in time for supper. Were up 10 hours and on oxygen for 8. Had about enough gas left to fill up a Chevrolet when we got back. . .

Ed and I are waiting for doc to come back so we can ask to go to Rome. . .

Italy
Oct. 15,

. . .We all have colds around here. Can't

help it. No matter what we do to prevent it, the dampness gets you. . . Haven't a stove yet, tho we're trying to get one made. . .

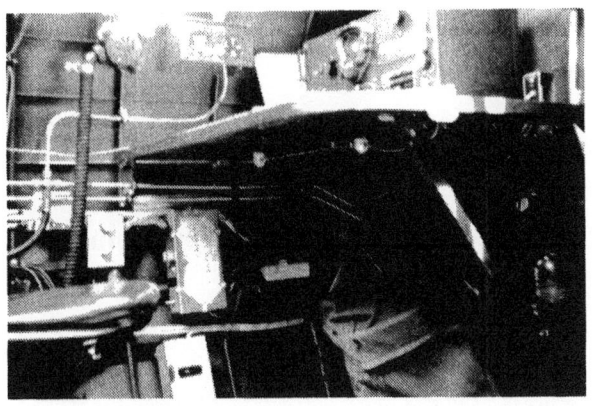

Radio room. Top photo shows desk and receiver, oxygen, interphone and heated suit connections. Bottom photo shows transmitter against rear bulkhead.

26. Potty Training

October 16,--Brux, Czechoslovakia. Large oil refinery--results unknown because of undercast. Flak intense, but not accurate in our sqd'n. Bombed by P.F.F. I send in bombing report. 0900.

P.F.F. was another designation for Mickey bombing. Our squadron flew Able Box and our crew led the squadron, so that put us in the front position in a Mickey ship. A colonel from group rode in the right-hand pilot's seat on this mission to a big synthetic oil plant in the Sudetenland. As lead radio operator I sent the coded bomb-drop report as soon as we released our load. The message provided the time, the target and results. For the latter the message said, "unknown."

Only half an hour or so after we left the target the colonel popped into the radio room, using a walk-around oxygen bottle. He appeared in misery and wanted to know what had happened to the "goddam relief tube." The rest of us had noticed its absence at the rear of the bomb bay. Ground crewmen probably had removed the simple rubber hose and funnel contraption during repairs.

To compensate, those of us who needed it had fallen back on the emergency container used universally by ground and air forces everywhere: empty K-ration boxes. I offered mine to the colonel and yelled at him to be sure after filling it to drop it, and not pour it, out the waist door.

Colonels don't easily take instructions from sergeants. Anyway, he reappeared in a couple of minutes, drenched and looking as if he could eat me for lunch. As he disappeared on his way forward the Mickey operator, a few feet away, spanked my shoulder and said, "Served him right." Grove later told me the officer had tried to pour the box's contents out the door but the slipstream whipped everything back in his face.

As we flew down the Adriatic that day we heard radio reports of low clouds covering our base. When we arrived somewhere off the Gargano spur the colonel ordered squadrons to break off and each pilot to find our base on his own. Then he called me on the interphone and ordered me to ask our base for a QDM, a bearing to fly to reach the strip. That would be silly because we weren't more than 40 miles from home. By the time the base operator could give us a bearing and it was relayed to him in the cockpit the bearing would have been useless.

So, forgetting for a moment the vast difference in our ranks, I blurted this advice into the interphone:

"Just tune your compass set to New York base and zero the needle."

Tuning to our base frequency would cause his cockpit radio compass needle to point to the base. Turning the plane then so the needle pointed straight up, at zero, would bring us over the base in minutes.

Serious second thoughts came to me as soon as the colonel got this little lesson in radio navigation. He might snatch back my new Tech Sergeant rank within hours. He never peeped, however, at least over the interphone. We landed without incident, and a Jeep driver whisked our colonel away.

The crew's four officers were doubled up in laughter as I carried my flight bag around to the front of the plane that day. Skok asked me if I always took on colonels in the style they had just witnessed. He didn't know the half of it, I said, and described my attempt to potty train the poor fellow.

Italy
Oct. 16,
7 P.M.

Just finished another long, hard day. Yep, I think I'll get me another kind of job when this is over. . .

Wish it (mail) would come over as fast as we came. . . Air travel is sure a wonderful thing. Makes me mad to think all these airplanes were made for war. . .

Italy,
Oct. 17, '44

. . .went over in a Jeep to get our laundry. Also drew one of the new field jackets and a sweater from supply. They are pretty nice.

Grove and Kleiber are outside frying some spuds again tonite. They have a homemade gas stove in the ground. . . We are still sweating out a stove for our tent. . . Still quite warm during the days if it doesn't rain.

Lots of guys always going home, and lots

more coming in from the States. We feel like old
timers now, and are too. We talk to them about the
old tough ones that are finished now, and know
darn well that there are still a lot of hard ones
left. . .

Italy,
Oct. 18

. . .Am sending a clipping with this. I know
all of the fellows in the story--especially Powell,
and was on the trip too. Have flown in old Pistol
Packin' Mama. . .She's sure done her share. They
are going to retire her as being "war weary."

The Stars and Stripes clipping told about one of our
planes. Flak had caused an oxygen flare-up, which always
seemed awful but rarely was. Six in the crew, including the
pilot, had bailed out. The rest, noticing that the fire had
burned out and that the plane had stabilized by itself, flew it
home.

Italy,
Oct. 19

. . . Rain-rain go away! Test hop this
afternoon--that's all. . .
A fellow was just in here with a spray bomb
killing mosquitos. . .

The next day, the 20th, the Sixth Army invaded the
island of Leyte in the Philippines.

Italy
Oct. 21
7 P.M.

. . . Tonight we have our stove up and going full blast. Sure feels good. We have a 50 gal. drum of gasoline outside, and a tube running in under our floor to the stove. (Drawing of stove included in letter.)

We also made a couple more writing tables and a new door for the tent. About ready for winter now. . .

Didn't write last night because I had to pull guard duty from 6 til 10. Sure a cold, lonesome job.

A drum of 100 octane gasoline lasted about a week in heating our tent. When we had used up the drum we unhooked the flexible pipe and rolled the barrel across the road to the fuel bunker and traded it for a full one. The stove, about a third of a steel drum itself, burned the gasoline as it dripped slowly into a little pot of rocks. Without pressure, the fuel didn't burn efficiently, so at least once a day we had to beat on the stovepipe to clear out the soot.

We had contrived relatively snug living quarters, nevertheless. Several steel bomb-tail crates made stools, cushioned by seat pads from parachute harnesses. All of us had scrounged wooden boxes for writing tables and to hold our personal junk. I stored my socks and skivvies in a steel crate that had been made for mortar shells.

Nobody liked the loneliness of guard duty. We presumed that our solitary march around the squadron's perimeter had a purpose: to challenge and keep out wandering Italians. That logic broke down, however, because about 20

Italian men, mostly discharged from Mussolini's army, lived and worked with us.

Still in their Italian army uniforms, these "Paisanos" cut our hair, cleaned our clothes and substituted for Kitchen Police in exchange for food from our mess shack. They slept in their own shelters and performed any odd jobs that came along. Ground crewmen in several tents at about this time hired groups of these former servicemen to build little huts of soft stone, called tufa. Each man's share of a hut's cost came to about $100. Our mechanics knew they'd probably remain through the winter, so they sought a bit of comfort. The huts, measuring about 12-by-18 feet, had fireplaces and corrugated iron roofs.

October 23,–Pilsen, Czechoslovakia. Skoda Munitions Works. Results unknown because of undercast. Flak intense and very accurate--our ship being pretty riddled. Had both main generators out and main tanks and batteries full of holes. Landed without brakes, so had to cut off diagonally across the field to keep from ramming other ship. 0920.

I flew that mission without a parachute. It happened because of having to double as a photographer. We flew deputy lead, Baker position in Able Box, the plane which had to photograph the bomb-strike. A big Fairchild K24 camera sat in the middle of the radio room when we arrived at the plane that morning.

To get the clumsy thing out of my way while we circled and formed up, I pulled out the floor section and stuck the camera in its mounting well. I shouldn't have opened the little camera door in the plane's fuselage. When I unzipped my flight bag and dumped its contents on the right side of the radio room, my parachute pack tumbled into the well and out the opening.

I missed it. My parachute habits had changed the day I learned of Charley Grayson's experience. Since then my chute pack got snapped onto my harness before we entered flak areas, even though it meant hanging the flak vest over the top and giving me the profile of a pregnant whale.

Not having a chute shouldn't have worried me much. If we had to bail out I could have snapped my harness to rings on someone else's harness, thereby sharing his canopy. That would have given us both a hard landing, but we often weren't in a position to be particular.

We knew when we landed that day that we didn't have any brakes. It relieved us to learn that we still had air in our tires. Halfway down the runway Skok started turning aside to avoid another plane still on the strip. We started bouncing as we crossed the other strips and then the perimeter track. Skok kicked rudder pedals and blasted the outboard engines to steer around taxiing and parked planes. Then we simply bounced along until we stopped, several hundred feet onto the grass.

A meat wagon pulled up as we jumped out, anxious faces wondering if we needed help. Then the S2 Jeep arrived and I handed over the camera's film magazine, though the sergeant already knew that clouds had prevented photography. A tug arrived next to pull our plane back to its hardstand, but we in the crew had to wait for several minutes for a ride.

Italy
Oct. 24

Yesterday I was on one of those long
9-hour sorties that leaves a person exhausted...
So Bob's outfit is operational now. Do you
suppose they will go out of the states?...
Sure nice to be able to relax when you're
tired. We talk for hours about religion, history,
geography, travel, etc. Lots of offered opinions...

On that day the Battle of Leyte Gulf opened in the Philippines with destruction of a Japanese naval force in Surigao Strait.

Italy
Oct. 25

Flood and I went into town today... Saw
Bing Crosby in "Going My Way."... We don't have
to pay to see shows either here at Group or in town.
The Red Cross has a large theater and a little
theater. and ENSA has one for the Limeys. That's
their USO I guess. The Salvation Army has their
setup in Manfredonia.
I got a cholera booster shot today and it's
made my arm stiff tonite...
We will take sulfa-diazine tablets for
combatting colds, meningitis, etc. The Doc is sure
a swell Joe--having been here in the outfit longer
than any other...

Italy
Oct. 26
7 P.M.

*A rainy day. . . and general mud controls
the field. . . We sit around the fire and read or just
talk and crack almonds & eat apples. We have a
little library set up. . . If we didn't do something
like that, our English and grammar would take
a beating because of the limited scope of
conversation, etc. . . . You can tell it in the fellows
who have been overseas a couple of years. . .*

*Ed and I saw the Doc today and he is going
to see about us going to Rome around the first of
Nov. . . .*

*There have been some infantry observers
flying with a few bomber crews lately, and some
air crew men on detached service up at the front.
They've finally decided that war is war and terrible
wherever you are. We get along pretty swell with
the ground forces around here.*

The little exercise in exchanging air and ground
troops didn't prove much. Public relations folks probably
dreamed it up. Each group concluded that it didn't like the
kind of war the other had to fight.

Forces of the British Empire formed most of the
ground troops around us in our part of Italy. A searchlight
company bivouacked along the road to Manfredonia, its
platoons spread among the surrounding airfields. Nobody
could divine their purpose, because we never used the
searchlights. Several other British units, usually detached in
some way, camped within 20 miles. The British notoriously
spread little units about for special projects and we rarely
unraveled their mysteries, but they let us hitch-hike in their
lorries.

After Ploesti disappeared as a target RAF squadrons switched to bombing Austrian and German targets--always at night, and usually cities. Several Vickers Wellingtons blew up that fall as they circled for altitude, creating concussions that shook our tents and trees. Wellingtons couldn't match the RAF's Halifaxes and B24s in performance, and we heard reports that a loaded Wellington couldn't climb over the Alps. One of them crashed into our squadron bivouac area on April 17, before we arrived, killing five mechanics and injuring a sixth.

Italy
Oct. 27
7 P.M.

Rainy day again. Just had a practice run in the afternoon. . . Usually read a whole book in one day if it's good.
Went into town with Lasota a while back and he found a bookstore where he bought a portfolio of old Italian art reproductions. . . .Have known him since I first got to S. Falls. . . Maybe we'll stroll down the Wilhelmstrasse together some day. . .

Italy
Oct. 29

. . . Picked up Lasota and we went to a town (San Severo) we hadn't been to before. Smaller, but cleaner than ours. . .
The war?--I think if it wasn't for weather, the war in Europe would be over by the 1st of Dec.

Italy
Oct. 31, 1944
9 A.M.

Sure wish the weather would let up. . .
We've put off our trip to Rome again. Can't go 'til we finish now. . .
What do you think of my going to school when I get out of the Army? Fellows not in are getting an education and I don't want to be a dumbell (sic).
It rained last night and it's slimey (sic). . . Almost broke my neck getting to and from supper . . .This life is easy but not winning the war very fast. . .

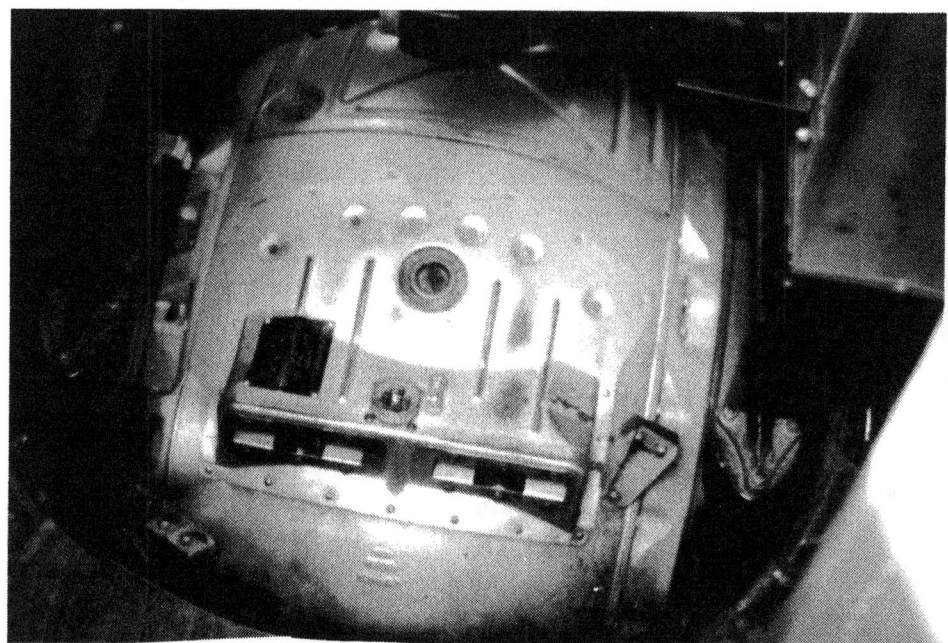

Outside of ball turret, from inside the plane.

27. Roman Holiday

Italy
Nov. 1

*. . . You talked about frying up all the
pheasant for those people. Wish I could have a
whole fried pheasant to chew on. Our supper was
beyond description. Had some pretty good apples
today tho. . .*

*The weather was OK for a change today. I
wasn't one of the lucky ones tho so it didn't do me
any good. Guess I'll stay at 37 for the duration.
Flood and Grove and Skok are ahead of me, but
Dick and Hall are way behind. . .*

*Draper (the 5th man in the tent) finished
up today. . .*

Italy
Nov. 2

*. . .Tonite, Ed Flood and I found that we
are scheduled to go to Rome to Rest Camp
tomorrow. It was some surprise after they told
us that we couldn't go 'til we had finished. We are
packing one bag. . . may leave early in the morning.
There are plenty of things to see and do in Rome,
so I'll tell you all about it when I get back. . .*

Will try to write while in Rome, but if not--don't worry. . .

Four officers and 10 enlisted men left our squadron early the next morning, the officers according to protocol in a personnel carrier and the rest of us in a covered six-by-six. A similar group left from 341st Squadron. Gears whining all the way, our truck rumbled through Benevento, Caserta and Cassino. Although we paused a few minutes to marvel at the devastation in Cassino, otherwise we didn't see much but wet trees and mountains. In the afternoon a light rain began to fall and a dirty mist from the truck's wheels invaded the open rear. In defense, we buttoned our raincoats together and hung them to create a barrier.

By late afternoon our truck rolled past the Colosseum and continued north to AAF Rest Camp 74 on the Via Veneto. In its usual spartan determination the Army had taken over several large buildings and provided a mess hall, cots and blankets. Flood and I and the rest ate and turned in early, resolving to look for more stylish quarters the next day. We hadn't come all this distance to sleep on cots.

Ed and I found what we wanted at the Albergo Regno on the Corso Umberto. This little hotel for about $4 a day gave us easy access to the Forum, Piazza Venezia, Trevi Fountain and Pantheon. Its elevator had failed and its water ran cold, but we slept gratefully on mattresses and sheets, and delighted in a little balcony over the Corso. We sat there tranquilly one evening enjoying the city, our discarded cigar butts making red arcs to the pavement. We couldn't help but revel in a world distinctly removed from our soggy little tent at Amendola.

The two of us tramped through the Colosseum, Circus Maximus and Forum, taking pictures of each other in

Hadrian's Arch. We caught a ride south on the Via Appia to the catacombs of S. Sebastian. We required an entire day to see St. Peter's cathedral, the Sistine Chapel and the Vatican galleries.

The allied military governments had brought to Rome hundreds of valuable art pieces from the rest of occupied Italy, both to protect them and to allow servicemen like us to see them on display in the Palazzo Venezia, which had been Benito Mussolini's palace. These works impressed me much more than the Vatican collection.

Within a few days Flood and I encountered Sgt. George Gable and several others who had traveled to Rome with us. Gable, a ground crew chief, announced that they had rented an entire floor of an apartment building. They had lots of space, they said, and invited us to move in, so within an hour we became apartment dwellers in a wealthy district near the Tiber River.

The others, especially the ground crewmen, had experience at rest leaves, and had brought with them coffee, canned preserves, pressed meat and even Army bread. They had talked the apartment manager into brewing coffee and frying our Spam every morning for a communal feast. Because most Romans hadn't tasted real coffee for a year or more, these good folks would do anything to share a cup. They wouldn't even allow us to throw out the grounds.

The city of Rome, free of the Jerries only since June, had barely begun to function again. The allied military government provided law and order and supervised the reopening of businesses. Servicemen on leave from the Air Forces and Fifth and Eighth Armies, their pockets full of lira, provided most of the business.

Few trattori or ristoranti had won approval, undoubtedly to protect our health. The military government did open two eating places during our stay early in November, supplying the food to guarantee its quality. We paid about 25 cents each for dinner tickets honored at the restaurants.

All of us got around on foot, mostly, or in open, horse-drawn carriages. Flood and I tried an auto/taxi on the first day, and the driver tried to charge us $10, so we refused to pay him anything. Walking let us set the pace but it wore us out after a day or two. We spent one disappointing evening at the British forces' Alexander Club, which offered us little entertainment but mass singing, and provided no refreshments but tea and coffee. One could tell that we were spoiled.

We visited some fancy stores and bought a few small things for gifts, but war had depleted stocks in the stores and inflation had swelled the price of clothing. Some of the best goods on sale were those that had been dumped by the Germans just before they pulled out. One stationery store, for example, displayed a 35mm Leica camera and all accessories for $25. It tempted me, but I had brought only about $75 with me and didn't want to run short. I need not have worried. We could trade cigarets, razor blades or soap for almost anything.

I had never seen anything like the open bazaars and flea markets. We couldn't pass one of these impromptu merchants without being offered the moon for our fountain pens --or shoes. Bartering ruled the day and the best "horse traders" could set themselves up for life. A few GIs obviously had caught the bug, because we heard more than one American serviceman awkwardly screaming his Italian sales pitch through a Midwestern accent.

Political speakers of various stripes held forth on nearly every corner. These opportunists recognized that power and influence begged the plucking. Although the war had not devastated their city it had wrecked the lives of many Romans. A good number nevertheless wore their frayed white shirts and frock coats with dignity. Weary of war, they could only look ahead. Having gained some security at last, they tolerated their new occupiers mostly because of our temporary status, and our lira.

Neither Flood nor I had tasted espresso or cappuccino coffee. A handful of small coffee bars had opened in Rome's central district, and residents, long deprived of their favorite brew, lined up for the tiny cups. After a taste, we decided that they didn't know beans about coffee. Its preparation, on the other hand, with all its attendant noise and flourishing of valves, kept us entranced.

The Foggia area's limited quantities and quality in wine and liquor made us appreciate a brandy we found in Rome's little street stalls or bistros. We soon stocked our apartment rooms with all descriptions of fancy drink. We could find little wine we liked, though, and blamed the Germans, assuming that they had taken it with them.

We learned one day that Armed Forces Radio in Algiers would broadcast the Army-Navy football game, so we scouted widely for a receiver. Then the apartment house owner heard of our interest and invited our whole gang to use the radio in her quarters on the top floor. On game day we supplied the coffee and some food. The Signora, who was in her sixties, provided wine and a lavishly decorated setting. She obviously enjoyed the party, and although the two football teams surely played, nobody remembered the game.

Our orders for rest camp had specified five days, but we knew we could stretch that because air groups sent trucks to Rome only when they could bring new loads of "restees." After five days we checked regularly at the Via

Veneto office for our transportation, and on the 10th day we learned that we'd catch our truck the next morning. Trying to wring all I could from the trip, I spent my last afternoon in Rome wandering alone through its markets and narrow streets. Next morning we settled up with the apartment manager and delighted him and his family by leaving a stock of coffee and canned marmalade.

During our return ride to Amendola we grew more conscious than usual of the cold, the damp and the hard wooden seat. We spoke only rarely, all of us no doubt regretting the end of our leave. Still, we couldn't help but feel renewed and rested.

Italy
Nov. 16, 1944

Just got back from Rome day before yesterday. I had 40 letters and 5 Oakes Times waiting for me. . .

Dale Dolton is missing in action. The ship he was on that day just didn't return and nobody seems to know what happened to it. We all hope that he is OK somewhere as he's sure a swell guy.

Am sending along a picture I had taken on top of St. Peter's Basilica. . . .

Dolton's plane had gone down during a mission to Salzburg, Austria, on Nov. 11. The group lost four planes that day, two because of a collision, though no flak was reported over the target. I'm not certain about Dolton's fate. Phil Skok informed the rest of us in the crew the next spring that he had learned that Dolton had been found alive by

British forces in Italy. But squadron records as late as 1993 show Dolton as killed in action.

On Nov. 16 the U.S. Ninth and First Armies opened their drive to clear the Roer River Plain.

The author, on roof of St. Peter's.

28. Winter Blahs

Italy,
Nov. 17, '44

. . . Skok finished up yesterday. He's been busy flying squadron lead and so kinda left us in the dust. Now that our pilot is finished, the 6 of us left will have to shift for ourselves on any crew that has a vacancy. I don't think there will be any trouble getting thru tho.

That ship that the clipping was about finally didn't come back yesterday. Guess old "Pistol Packin' Mama" won't pack any guns anymore.

I'll be doggonned. Hall just said she came in today--with 3 men on her. Looks like the old lady will outlive all the crews here. The crews flying some of these ships give up before the planes do. . .

Three in "Mama's" crew had brought her back to Ancona, made some repairs and returned to our base the next day.

Squadron Operations managed to keep the remaining six of us together as much as possible, filling in the gaps with others on most missions.

. . . I made a false start this morning.
Something went wrong, so I had another day of
vacation. Will try again tomorrow. . .

November 19—Vienna, Austria. Winterhaven oil
storage dump. We bomb thru solid undercast by
P.F.F. and see black smoke columns billow up
thru it. Very intense flak barrage covering about
25 miles, but it is not accurate in our group. 0715

I had been standing at the gun position and as the bombardier announced, "bomb doors open," I turned around for my usual bombs-away check. The inside of the plane crystallized before my eyes. Or, rather, my eyes crystallized. In a fit of carelessness I had forgotten to pull my goggles down, and the moisture on my eyes froze in an instant. Once the goggles went in place the frost melted. A few minutes later I could see well enough to report that the bombs had dropped, but the rims of my eyelids stayed red for several days.

Sixteen planes reported minor damage that day. About 30 minutes after we left the target on the way home, Flood reported a fighter approaching slowly from the rear. He couldn't identify it, so our pilot told him to fire a burst over it. The fighter pilot immediately banked a bit to display his profile. We saw a P38, one prop feathered and a big chunk bitten from its stabilizer.

Even on one engine the plane slowly overtook our group and pulled directly under us, about 50 feet away. The plane's nose showed no gun ports, so we figured it was a camera or weather plane, probably hit by flak. The pilot's wave indicated he was OK, but he clearly wanted our protection on the way home. In his position safety could become tantalizingly elusive. As we reached a point about 50 miles north of our base he waved again and peeled off.

After gun cleaning that day I had to sweep bits of cheese out of the radio room. To keep their contents from freezing, we normally stuffed our K-ration boxes into the shin pockets of our coveralls, but on this day my little waxed box had been overlooked. When I opened it and jabbed a knife into the cheese it shattered like glass.

Italy
Nov. 19

   . . . Thought we were going to have it pretty rough today, but it turned out to be quite an easy one. . .

   Got your clipping about the 15th A.F. and what happened to Ploesti. We (crew) were on 4 of those 19 missions. If anything will have been the decisive factor in the war over here, that stands a good chance of being it. . .

Italy
Nov. 20, '44

   . . . Sure seems like everyone I know is in the thick of it and getting hurt. Hope Maynard wasn't hurt too bad. . .

   Nailed some pasteboard on my wall to help keep out the cold and lined the bottom of my cot to the same purpose. . .

Maynard Furan, inducted with me, became a casualty on Oct. 11, my birthday. He was in a 1st Division mortar crew south of Aachen and a piece of shrapnel hit him in the hand. Within days medics evacuated him to England and then to the States.

Italy
Nov. 21,
7 P.M.

Nothing to do all day but read and eat. . .
Ed is off on a Jukin' trip to Caserta, so we
are just 3 in the tent.

Everybody looked for an excuse to go to Caserta. The Fifth Army made its headquarters in a castle there. We found the food and accommodations splendid if shameful.

Italy
Nov. 23,
6 P.M.

Thanksgiving day, and what a swell day it's
been, too. . . we had a complete holiday. Breakfast
was from 8 to 9 instead of from 7 to 8, and our
Thanksgiving dinner was from 3:30 to 5:30. . . We
had turkey (roasted), m. potatoes. dressing, peas.
gravy, relish, caulliflower (sic), pie, peaches,
coffee and almonds. . .
Flip (Skok) will be leaving as soon as he
gets his orders. Did I tell you he got the D.F.C.?
(Distinguished Flying Cross). He sure deserves it. .

223

Italy
Nov. 24

Well, we're back on the old diet. Spam and hash for dinner. . .

On that day 11 B29s attacked Tokyo from new air bases built in the recently captured Marianas Islands.

Italy
Nov. 25.

. . . This finicky weather sure isn't helping us win the war. . .
Ed got (in a package) cans of shrimp, crab, sardines, tuna. . . etc. Pretty nice to open of a nite when you get hungry. We can pick up bread at the mess tent. . .

Italy
Nov. 26,

. . . Still cloudy and cool in the daytime and getting colder every nite. . .
How is the hunting? . . . Some of the fellows here get some carbines and a jeep and drive up into the mountains & hunt deer. They haven't done so well so far, but they say there is a lot of game. I guess the deer are too fast. . .

Italy
Nov. 27

Lasota came over after dinner today, and we went into town and bummed. . .

Did I tell you about Doug Clarke? (S. Falls, Yuma, R. City). Well, after he finished about 15 missions here, he got a chance to fly as Radioman on Gen. Twining's private ship. Permanently. He's been all over this theater and back to the States several times. A pretty good thing, altho I imagine he has to take a lot of baloney. . .

Doug Clarke got his job because he was from Wisconsin and Gen. Twining wanted an all-Wisconsin crew. They flew in a B17 that had been stripped of turrets and guns. A rebuilt interior included bunks in the bomb bay.

Italy
Nov. 28

. . .Received 2 boxes in pretty good shape. . . you sure hit the nail on the head with everything you sent. . .

Same schedule. . . I am content to hold out here until spring. . .we can do almost as we want. . .

Italy
Nov. 29.

I walked down to the 340th Squadron to see Lasota. . . We sat and talked and ate his Christmas candy and cookies. . .we came back to my squadron and ate some of my stuff until time for the show (6:30). The film broke twice, one bulb burned out and the thing wouldn't focus, but we got the main parts. . .

Charley was kinda disgusted because his "battle scars" were disappearing. He said he wanted something to back up his yarns when he gets to be an old man. He was wounded slightly in the arm one day. His pilot put him in for the Purple Heart, but I don't think he even went to the dispensary. . .

Italy
Nov. 30,

. . . Wish the rain would let up. . .

We were paid this afternoon. I'll send another $200 home tomorrow. . . Maybe I can save up enough. . .to get through college--if I don't forget all I ever knew first. . .

These C-Rations we get shouldn't happen to a dog. They seem to be able to can anything. . .

29. A Potent Brandy

Italy
Dec. 2
6:30 P.M.

     . . . The outfit was busy, but I wasn't in
on it. Same deal tomorrow. We have a lot of new
men coming in and they fly them instead of us. . .
     We are sure in a fix now for lights at night.
We can't even get any candles now. I'm writing
this by the light of our gasoline stove. . .
     First Sg't. was just in here saying we might
have to find room for a couple of the new guys
in our tent. . .

This influx of new crews, combined with poor weather, continued to restrict our flying. We let the Operations officer know we'd fly with anybody, anytime.

Italy
Dec. 3

     Another pretty nice day. Wish I could be
lucky enough to take advantage of it. These new
crews are getting all of the breaks. . .
     Flip (Skok) left for home this morning. He

said he would probably spend Christmas at sea. . .
    Still no candles. . . it's only 4:30 and
already getting dark.
    Grove flew again today. He has 48 now.
Dick (Mabie) has checked out as first pilot and
we will fly with him.--But he left for Rest Camp
again this morning. . . Maybe we can fill in with
another crew. . .

                                        Italy
                                        Dec. 4

    . . . This mud is sure awful. . . The ground
has been lived on for so many thousands of years
that it isn't dirt anymore. It's just decayed--
everything. . .

A gift from a departing friend at about this time
warmed me in a couple of ways. Ordered home after completing his missions, this guy, a navigator, brought me an
eiderdown comforter which originally had lined a sleeping
bag. It folded lengthwise and provided a most luxurious
sack, substituting for about 40 pounds of blankets and coats
that I had piled on my cot.

                                        Italy
                                        Dec. 5,

    Has Bob moved again? . . . Hope he gets
somewhere where it is at least civilized. This place
is just civilized. The only bad thing is the weather.
Chow is passable, and we have our tent fixed up
just the way we want it. Better than Army life back

in the States. . .

After the weather changed and we could no longer enjoy the lido, we moved our attention and our visits to Foggia. Day by day, the town provided more attractions, including a couple of bistros. Quite often we'd catch a ride in mid-afternoon, visiting the Red Cross first to check on new developments. Then, after finding something to eat, we often settled on one of the little bars.

These places couldn't get much drinkable goods. The Army checked them constantly because their owners tried at times to sell a poisonous brandy made with wood alcohol. Nevertheless, we found some anise-based liquor one night, called strega, that knocked our socks off. Trouble was, we couldn't rid ourselves of its licorice flavor for days.

Partly in self-defense, our mess officer and squadron cook set up a bar in one end of the mess shack. A parachute was hung and spread from the ceiling to reflect the light, and nearly every night an old upright piano attracted singers and an accompanist.

In his sorties through the countryside the cook had uncovered stocks of a fair cherry brandy. He appealed to all of us for donations of very sour grapefruit juice which we bought each week at the PX tent. Mixed with the syrupy brandy, it produced an acceptable drink--frothy and pink to be sure, but both savory and potent. Anyone who dawdled late at the bar needed escort through the mud to the security of tent and cot. Before planning an entire evening at the brandy, however, a wise crewman checked first to see if he had been scheduled to fly the next day.

Italy
Dec. 6,

4 P.M.

. . . Still I'm not on the list. . . Tuck is out flying today. they are all ahead of me but Hall and Mabie. . .

Tuck just came in--he spent a long hard day with nothing to show for it. . .

Italy
Dec. 7,
4 P.M.

(It was) Just 3 years ago this afternoon when we heard the news about Pearl Harbor. Lots of things have happened since then. . . Would have been a junior in college now. . . As it is, we've all just wasted our time fighting instead of living & learning. . .

Rained again today. We just sit around and read. I finish a book nearly every other day.

About this time a couple of new, soot-colored B17s arrived in every group. The brass in Bari called them "intruder" ships. They flew individually at night and instead of bombs they carried extra fuel so that their sorties lasted 12 hours or so. They criss-crossed German-occupied Europe, hoping to disrupt the enemy war effort by stirring incessant air-raid alarms. Special crews arrived with the planes, so we never became involved.

Italy
Dec. 8,

. . . We walked down to the farm house this afternoon and got our laundry. It costs us about a dollar a week for that. Rations (at the PX) come to about $1.50 a week, and haircuts cost a dime. . .

Dick is still in Rome. We have to sweat him out, I guess, before we can finish. . . we are getting the short end. They can all go jump in the lake--we can stay here 'til spring. . .

In addition to laundry service, this family who farmed about a mile northeast of our squadron area would sell us wine--a pint bottle for a pack of cigarets. I usually picked up a bottle of marsala, a heavy Sicilian cooking wine that appeared to be a better quality than most.

Italy
Dec. 9,

. . . A late mail came in last night, and I got a letter from you, one from Bert, and one from Maynard. . .

Maynard was still in the hosp. . . Said his left hand was torn up some. . .

Grove finished today. He has been flying while the rest of us have been sitting around. Guess he will be going home soon. . .

Took a good long shower this morning and then shaved. . . My beard is getting rougher, but I still don't shave only every third day. ha.

Italy
Dec. 10,

Today was a break in the monotony. . . We were finally on the list, but again the weather brought us back. Just a whole morning of hard work for nothing. . .

I used to like to listen to rain falling on a roof, but after living in a tent in the rain for so long, it isn't so nice.

Chow is still pretty rough. . . We just go in and eat and wait 'til afterwards for the discussion of what it was that we had. It always tastes better when the put-put is broken down so the lights are out. . .

The rain is really roaring against the old tent. This old tent has gone thru about 3 entire campaigns and sure shows it. It still carries frag holes from Tafaraoui and the mud of every section of Italy. . .

These recalled or aborted missions made us more bitter than any other kind, especially when we had waited three weeks. I picked up the message from our base to the lead ship, calling us back, and hated to relay the news to the pilot and crew. All our preparations that day already had cost us five hours of work and discomfort, and three hours remained before we could relax. By this time none of us needed the practice.

30. Rocks and Lice

December 11—Vienna, Austria. Moosbeirbaum oil refinery northwest of Vienna on Danube R. We bomb visually thru heavy smoke screen. Three large columns of smoke seen rising from target area. Very heavy flak and quite intense— even at our 29,000 ft. altitude. Are potted by flak batteries at Gyor and another town on the way home. Temperature about 50 below zero. No fighters seen.

I wrote that notebook entry about five days later, after returning from Yugoslavia. We were a bastard crew for that Vienna mission and none of us remembered many hits on our plane over the target, though 23 planes reported damage. We decided later that fire from the 88mm batteries on the way back must have caused most of our own damage. Somewhere between Maribor and Zagreb, Yugoslavia, the right waist gunner reported a heavy loss of fuel from our right tanks. Through my right window it looked to me more like steam than liquid. The co-pilot checked the gauges and reported that we had lost almost all of our gasoline from the main tanks in the right wing. Although most flak holes in our fuel cells were self-sealing, we had learned that some jagged rips never closed.

The pilots waited until our two engines on the right had used all their fuel before having more transferred from left wing tanks. Perhaps we could have flown home without No. 3 and No. 4 engines, but it would have been tricky, and the pilots decided to try to keep them going. That meant, however, that part of every gallon transferred would leak away into the air. The navigator worked out our range and gave us the bad news: Even if we could burn every remaining gallon we wouldn't make it past the Adriatic coast.

The pilot, whom I had never met before, described our situation to the squadron leader, indicating that we'd find a place to land--or bail out. The lead pilot told him to maintain our course as long as possible in order to give people at our group base a better idea of our location when we landed. Soon after that we dropped out of formation, starting a steady descent and trying to fly as far as we could.

Not much later the pilot announced that he had picked out a place to put the plane down. He said he preferred a crash landing rather than having everybody bail out. Then we began to circle and lost more altitude as the engineer and co-pilot kept our right engines turning over. We had about 500 feet between us and the hills when the pilot told everybody but the co-pilot to go to the radio room and get ready for a hard landing.

As the rest crowded into my little room I got our position from the navigator and sent it to New York base in code. The others popped a couple of chute packs, filling our space with nylon fabric and riser lines. I had the only seat, and rotated it to the rear so I could brace my feet against the transmitter on the rear bulkhead. The other seven sat in rows like tobogganists, their backs to the front, and stuffed yards of parachute cloth around themselves.

The rest of us didn't know it, but by now our pilots had discovered that we'd land pretty hard, indeed. This wide, dry river bed they had picked for our landing strip turned out to be full of rocks as big as Jeeps. But because we had dropped too low to bail out and had lost or burned most of our fuel, they decided to bring the plane in, wheels up. As we made one final turn, some good-size hills on our left looked pretty close.

Our pilots cut the engine switches just before we hit, then everything on the plane started shuddering and banging. Shapes passed my window, sensed rather than seen. The plane appeared to strike several obstacles, wrenching us hard each time. Part of the left wing swung backward, but that's all I remember of the landing.

My next memory is of dust, swirling in the sunlight, and absolute silence. I appeared to be on my back in the bomb bay, looking upward at a big tear in the side. My feet were in the air, so I rolled over and discovered that my safety belt still held me to the radio seat. After releasing the strap I crawled through sand toward an opening at ground level.

As I emerged from under the plane just beside the No.3 engine, the co-pilot, sliding out his window, flopped on his rear almost beside me. Somebody else, one of the gunners, came out the same opening I had used. We could see somebody behind the wing, crawling away, and the co-pilot told us we'd better move away too, in case of fire. It took a couple of tries for me to stand because spasms repeatedly shook my legs.

Four of us quickly gathered and sat or lay within a few feet of the right wingtip. Then the pilot came around the front of the smashed fuselage and told us that some of the crew had been caught under the plane. We followed him to the other side where three men, the navigator, bombardier and a gunner, knelt beside the waist window, digging sand away from two who had been dragged under the ship.

Luckily, not much remained of the bottom of the fuselage, so the two men came out without any problem, one covered in blood and the other screaming when we moved one arm. The two apparently had been sitting in the middle of the radio room and had gone out the bottom. Something, probably rocks, had dragged away both the bomb bay doors and ball turret, clearing out most of the lower part of the plane.

Dragging in the sand had cut the gunner's scalp on one side and pulled it down, ear and all, nearly to his shoulder. Somebody found an emergency kit, and after powdering his scalp with sulfa, sand and all, we tied it roughly back in place with his scarf. He didn't seem to be in much pain and even helped attend to himself. The other man who had gone out the bottom of the radio room had a broken leg as well as a broken arm. Two guys set the arm but couldn't do much for his leg, then they taped pieces of ammo boxes to both limbs. The navigator had just jabbed morphine into our two injured crewmen when we saw our visitors.

They were two young men, each carrying a rifle, who had walked up as we attended to our injured. They both pointed down the valley, apparently the way they had come. Both wore green fatigue-style caps, adorned with a tin star at the front. Our pilot guessed that they probably were Partisans, though we couldn't understand their speech. After a minute or two one of them started trotting off in the direction they had pointed. We didn't pay much attention, but with a lot of struggling we moved our two injured men a few yards to the side of the wreckage.

Somebody near me suddenly rubbed the back of my neck and then showed me a streak of blood on his fingers. I reacted by making a swipe at my head and confirmed that I was, indeed, bleeding. Removing the helmet and its earphones, I soon found a little gash, which the co-pilot promptly salted with sulfa powder and stuck tape over it.

All of us now started examining ourselves more thoroughly, and everybody found a few cuts and bruises. One, who I think was the bombardier, complained of a severely sprained wrist. Most of us also realized that we still hadn't removed our parachute harnesses and Mae Wests, so when we relieved ourselves of those we moved better and felt better. We also kicked off our cumbersome sheepskin boots and started crawling through the wreckage to look for other clothing. It was probably about 1 p.m. when we landed and didn't seem cold, but we thought temperatures surely would drop after sundown.

The fuselage of our plane retained most of its original shape, but everything seemed to have broken loose in the landing. Guns and ammunition lay everywhere, one gun sticking into the bulkhead behind the radio room. Looking around us, we began to appreciate our luck, and the pilot's skill in avoiding boulders. My swivel bucket seat had broken loose from the plywood floor and somehow had crashed through the narrow bulkhead door, carrying me into the bomb bay. It occurred to me to burn my operator's flimsy, which gave all the code changes for the day, but I couldn't find it. An inertia switch had already destroyed the IFF radar identification equipment. The bombardier found and buried his bomb sight, although his orders specified that he should rescue it and carry the dumb thing to safety.

At about this time a feeling of wretchedness and hopelessness nearly overwhelmed me. The other nine may have felt the same, and it probably resulted from the shock of the landing and finding ourselves cut off from our usual contacts and comforts. We still faced too many unknowns, and the fact that we in this crew scarcely knew each other added to my desperation.

Our bruises had begun to pain us too by the time the second Partisan reappeared, this time with three or four helpers and two skinny mules. Immediately, they boosted our two injured gunners onto the animals and tied them down. Then, with appropriate signals for us to follow, they started at a fast pace down the creek bed. Our benefactors' eyes seemed to scan the ridges constantly, even though few Germans remained in all of the Balkans.

It may have been an hour and a half or two hours before we arrived at a rough cabin, built into the side of a hill. A loud, long Slavic argument, obviously about us, began between two people who appeared to us to be in command. Then, as it turned dark, the mule tenders started the two animals down the valley again. With a lot of gestures and pointing the two leaders convinced our pilot that our two casualties would be in the coastal town of Split by the next evening. We didn't envy them their cold ride on muleback.

Bailouts and forced landings had become so common in Yugoslavia by this period of the war that the Partisans and other friendly local groups had set up a business in shuttling crewmen back to Italy. Split and other coastal towns had fallen to them late in October. In return for every salvaged flier they could claim food, clothing and munitions, especially from the British. The value of these Partisan bands in helping to wage the war had disappeared along with the Germans. Now they mostly rescued airmen and fought Ustachi, the pro-German guerrillas, and anyone else they didn't like. They had our vote in any case.

Little of that first night remains in my memory. Somebody took us inside, and the cabin turned out to be a smelly but spacious cave, with what appeared to be old doors for a floor. Piles of straw attracted us and we collapsed, ignoring soreness and hunger. Exhaustion had overwhelmed all other demands but a yearning to sleep.

We awoke in the morning to a loud stomping on the floor boards. In semi-darkness a young man offered us tin cups, then a pair of very dirty hands extended a large bowl of steaming tea toward me. The owner of the hands nodded for me to take some, and as I dipped my cup I could see the same shades of filth on my own.

I never liked tea much until that day. Hot, strong and sweet, it seemed to flow through to my feet, glowing and energizing. The tea man left but then reappeared in a few minutes with loaves of bread which he broke into chunks and divided among us. We all chewed and swallowed as if we had discovered a new talent. Finally, taking time to look around us, we could see in the piles of straw eight or ten Partisans, two of whom appeared to be women.

My hair had matted in dried blood and straw, and I needed to wash my hands, face and scalp. So I joined several others who got to their feet and went outside, all of us groaning as we discovered new sore places and strained joints. My head and collar soon got a cold soaking in a trough of water at a rough corral, next to which lay six 50 cal. machine guns and a heap of ammunition belts and parachute packs. We speculated that our hosts had liberated them during the night from our wrecked ship. More power to them, we figured.

All that day we sat on the barren hillside, anxious to get moving, but the pilot got only cheerful gestures and smiles when he tried to convey our impatience. We might have set off on our own if we had even the slightest notion of where to go. That afternoon we repeated the tea and bread ration, still swallowing in haste as if we were starving.

Inside the cabin that night the tea bowl contained a thin, gray gravy, in which swam tiny pieces of meat. Goat, we thought, because we had noticed a few animals in the hills. Sitting on the floor, we all dipped chunks of bread into this viscous mix and gobbled it down. Nobody complained.

When the last of the bread had mopped up the last of the stew that night our bowl became a communal drinking font. One of the leaders of our Slavic rescue squad emptied a sizable jug of water-clear liquor into it, then dipped his tin cup. Motioning for all of us to follow his example, and holding his cup high, he offered a toast.

"Dravo!" Anyway, that's how it sounded.

All of us entered into this good-natured swilling, though the first swallow made me gasp. One of our officers identified our drink as slivovitz, a plum brandy notable for its skull-busting potential. I don't remember that I drank much, but also don't remember even lying down to sleep.

We started walking on the second morning, after trying as well as we could to thank our hosts. Three armed Partisans who seemed no more than 16 or 17 years old guided us, mostly southward.

All of us felt the cold. Nearly all had kept and still wore electric suits under our coveralls, but we could have used our insulated flying suits. None of us had kept the heavy gear in his flight bag because it wasn't necessary for missions, and we had chosen almost universally to use the pants and parkas for pillows and covers on our bunks--back in Italy.

I had found my fatigue cap and heavy gloves in the plane, and several crewmen tore strips of parachute about two feet wide and tied them around their waists. These turned out to be our salvation on two cold nights. In addition, we each carried a bottle of tea and several chunks of bread, which we stuffed in every available pocket.

For two days our path would take us down rough trails in a river bed for several miles and then carry us over rocky, evergreen-covered hills for a mile or two to another valley. We walked on sand in the river beds and sharp shale on the hills, sliding awkwardly much of the time. Our guides stopped for a few minutes every hour or two, but generally kept us hustling, obviously wanting to cover a lot of ground. On the first night we crawled into the edges of a strawstack to sleep.

The next day we saw people at several farms and a couple of villages before we reached the outskirts of Split. We never went into town, but instead our young Partisans led us down steep streets late on the second afternoon to a small stone wharf on the north edge of the city. There they took us to a boat and turned us over within minutes to two men who apparently had been waiting. Before our guides left, we embarrassed them with our salutes and by slapping them on their backs.

The boat which was to carry us away was about 30 feet long and obviously had been made for fishing. We had barely found places to sit in the rear when its engine started thumping and we pulled away. By then the sun had set and, as the small craft moved out between two islands, we started freezing. We might have perished that evening if we hadn't wrapped ourselves in nylon strips and lay together to share our warmth.

Luckily, our misery didn't last more than a couple of hours. We didn't pay much attention to where we were going, and were hardly aware when the little craft nosed into an inlet. We pulled up to a pier where a man switched on a flashlight and spoke a few words of English. Nothing could have raised my spirits more. Whatever the others thought about it, and despite our debt to the band in the hills, I had grown tired of Croatian, or whatever language we had heard for the past few days. Now we had landed on the island of Vis, and this fellow on the pier was a Commando in a small British force there.

As soon as we hauled our stiff bodies ashore he asked if any of us needed treatment, then led us quite a distance to a barracks-like shed. Inside, we warmed our chilled bones at a stove as somebody passed around a pan of biscuits and poured each of us a canteen cup of hot coffee. Warmth of the drink soon melted away much of my dejection, but few groups of men have presented such a bedraggled sight as the eight of us who stood near that heater. Blankets and cots awaited us, but only for two or three hours. The sergeant who met us at the pier said he expected a rescue boat at three a.m. One of our British saviors said this barracks and another just like it had been set up for the sole use of rescued crews like ours.

We pulled into the harbor at Bari around dawn. A Canadian rescue craft, a heated one this time, had carried us south across the Adriatic while we slept. All the stress of the past four days had built to a point beyond exhaustion. Once in Bari, we passed through a speedy interrogation, mostly to make clear which group of Partisans had helped us. We learned here that our two injured gunners had arrived safely and were being treated in the AAF hospital. Then we showered, deloused and got into fresh coveralls. We guessed that our tiny passengers, which had "bugged" us for the past two days, had come from Yugoslavian straw.

That morning, Dec. 15th, a plane from the 414th returned us to Amendola where we checked in at the Operations desk and learned that S2 had followed our movements all the way. A lieutenant told us not to worry: we hadn't been declared missing, and nobody had collected our gear from our tents. It had concerned all of us that missing-in-action reports might have been sent to our families. Crews in our squadron apparently had seen us land safely on the 11th, and the Partisan rescue link had developed so efficiently that nobody doubted our safe return. If only we had been as confident.

I slept eight or nine hours before going to chow. During the meal somebody told me I had been posted to fly the next day. I could scarcely believe it, but caught a ride to the crew equipment shack to be issued a new set of flying gear before dark.

31. It's Over

December 16—Linz, Austria. Benzol oil refinery in Linz. Briefed on Brux, Czecho, we bombed 2nd alternate because we were too late. Target just No. of Alps in heavy undercast, so we drop by P.F.F. Moderately heavy flak—very accurate, however we were untouched except for one hole. No fighters seen. 0710.

It's hard now to interpret ". . .we were too late." We may have arrived out of step with other groups assigned to attack Brux.

My new electrical suit heated more unevenly than the old one that had been discarded at the shower room in Bari. During this mission my feet turned numb again for several hours and I decided that something had to be done for them. The bulkhead wall ahead of my desk had been kicked so regularly that the thin aluminum bore a distinct depression. The ground crew chief pointed at the concave area one day and asked if I held a grudge against his airplane.

That evening after chow Doc Remley handed over some narrow strips of nylon parachute and told me to wrap them around my feet before pulling on the wool socks. On the mission roster for the next day were the names of all

244

that remained in my crew, giving me a chance to test the flight surgeon's idea.

Italy
Dec. 16, '44

> *. . . Today's trip made me 43. It wasn't so bad, altho I wouldn't have admitted it at the time. It's pretty easy, when it's over, to say--"Well, it was just another long ride." We had fresh fried eggs for breakfast early this morning, and I had a stomach ache all the way up. When the shootin' started I forgot about it. ha. . . . Don't worry--I'll take care of me.*

I had decided not to mention my recess in Yugoslavia--since no official notice had gone out. By the time the subject came up at home the war was over.

That was the day Field Marshal von Rundstedt sent three German armies loose against a lightly held U.S. line in the Ardennes, starting what came to be called the "Battle of the Bulge."

December 17--Blechhammer, Germany. North aviation gas plant. We bomb thru solid undercast, so cannot see results. Plenty of flak as usual, but not accurate in our group. Ed saw smoke drift up thru the undercast, so we must have hit something. 0900.

Italy
Dec. 17,

*Another busy day for us. I'm so tired now
I'm about to drop, and am afraid I will be more
tired tomorrow nite. . .*

*Today was a long, hard trip, but we got off
easy compared to the usual thing. . . Just about to
fall apart at the hinges. Guess I can't take it like
I used to. Wish they wouldn't bunch up like this. . .*

Strips of nylon helped my feet a little in the cold, but
they made my shoes too tight. Instead of being so stubborn,
I should have tied my shoes to my harness and simply added
more layers of wool socks inside the flying boots.

And after my long hiatus from flying I shouldn't have
complained about being scheduled, even for three days
straight.

**December 18—Odertal, Germany. Oil and gas
refinery 9 miles up the Oder River from
Blechhammer. Again we bomb thru solid
undercast and cannot see results. Moderate
flak and not close to our group. Landed with
very little gas. 8 fighters. 0830.**

The group lost one plane on that mission, and nobody could report why. About half of the planes left formation early on the trip home because they had run short of
fuel. On most of these missions in the fall and winter our
fighter escort saw little action as bomber cover, so as soon
as our wing leaders released them they peeled out of their
high sweeps and dived to the deck. They looked for German
trains and truck convoys, shooting up any military target

they could find. When we could see them through the clouds they provided a fine show far below.

Italy
Dec. 19, '44

> . . . *Just taking it easy today after 3 hard days. . . Washed up and shaved this A.M. There wasn't much time for that the past week. . .*
> *Ed finished up day before yesterday, and I am the only one in the tent who isn't finished. Tuk pulled his last one with us yesterday. Hall, Dick and I are the only ones left.*

Every time anyone in our crew completed his requir-ed number of missions, starting with Skok, we opened an-other bottle of the champagne we had bought in the Azores. We didn't mind its poor quality under the circumstances. My bottle remained under my cot, waiting.

> **December 20--Regensburg, Germany. Oil storage tanks near city. This was 2nd alternate. Brux, the primary was out because of weather. Again we bomb thru undercast by P.F.F. No results observed. No flak to speak of in our group. We were potted by flak at Passau, Austria. No fighters seen. Bomb run at 29,000 feet. 48 below zero. 0800.**

I sent in the bomb strike report that day. The lead radioman tried, but his weak signal indicated that his trans-mitter wasn't working right or he hadn't tuned it right. The alternate lead operator didn't wake up to the problem, so I coded a report and sent it. The group communications officer found me and thanked me that afternoon when I checked in my flimsy. We always had plenty of radio power. Using the 75-watt liaison transmitter, a radio operator could send a signal around the world from 29,000 feet.

Italy
Dec. 20,

Another hard day at work. . . Am glad it wasn't any longer. . . My feet were getting numb. . . had to really bang them around to keep the circulation up. . .

Received another package from you. . . I have 5 tubes of T. Paste now and about a ream of various kinds of stationary (sic). Am trading two tubes of T. Paste to Eskew for some things he has . . .Say, that hand lotion and lanolin is sure swell for my hands. They were awfully dry and cracking from the gas and oil. . .

I'm sure glad Dick checked out as first pilot. This way we all have a regular pilot to finish up with. Otherwise we would have to wait around and fly whenever some crew was short a man. I'd rather fly with Dick than anyone else anyway. Some of these guys couldn't drive a kiddie-car. . .

One of the other operators here is from N. Dak. Some little town up east of Devil's Lake. . . .Sure funny how you can meet people and live and work with them and not know much about them. . . I guess the Army specializes in that tho. Know 'em, and forget 'em is the saying. Wish I could. . . .

The skin on our hands dried and cracked as a result of our gun cleaning and because we often helped the ground crews scour dust and mud from the planes. Engine fairings and the wings just behind the engines gathered filth whenever the plane moved. Scrubbing with 100 octane gasoline took it off the aircraft, but did little for our hides and dispositions.

Italy
Dec. 21, '44

. . . This darn weather is about to drive me crazy. . . would like to see a good N. Dak. blizzard right now just for a little excitement. . .
The sqd'n is having a big blowout in town tonite, but as it is raining, Tuk and I decided to stay here. They usually turn out to be brawls anyway. . .
We had some toasted cheese sandwiches this afternoon. We got some bread at the mess shack and used the cheese from some K-rations. . .

Italy
Dec. 23,

Have been sitting around keeping the fire going as it has been pretty cold. . .
The news hasn't been so hot lately has it?

Stories about German advances in the Ardennes shocked and discouraged us. We had been primed for more

Allied advances to the Rhine and beyond. Now we envision-
ed a much longer war.

> *Italy*
> *Dec. 24,*

> *T'was the nite before Christmas and all thru*
> *the tent not a sad sack was stirring--not even a*
> *louse. . . No excitement whatsoever. . .*

> *Italy*
> *Christmas Day*
> *5 P.M.*

> *Just came from our Christmas dinner. . . I*
> *got about half of a turkey breast. . .*
> *It's been drizzling all day. . .*
> *The boys were out today--even in this*
> *weather. Don't imagine it was much fun at all. I*
> *hope to finish up on a nice day if I can.*

Our supply folks issued overshoes to about half of
us in November, so we shared the use of a couple of pair in
our tent. We left them near the door and cleaned them only
when the mud had grown too heavy to carry. For trips to
the shower tent we usually wore only a raincoat and overshoes, waiting to change to clean clothes on our return. We
slopped over to the mess tent in shifts so each of us could
protect his shoes, which had to be dry for flying.

The cruel bug of war struck digestive systems that
night. Cookie blamed it on the turkey dressing, which he de-
nied making. Miraculously, I escaped its ravages, but
throughout the night we could hear tent doors slamming

and sounds of anguish from desperate men competing for space in the latrines. Some didn't even make it as far as our covered johnnys. The "Black Corn," our mimeographed squadron newsletter, described the melee under the heading: "Missions We Don't Get Credit For." The story reported that some bombardiers had to salvo short of the target. A few officers, apparently anticipating a bad day, asked to be removed from the next day's mission roster.

> **December 26—Odertal, Germany. Synthetic oil refinery. We become separated from Sqd'n climbing through undercast. We are only ship in Sqd'n to find Group, and that is in N. Hungary. We bomb visually in good weather and put good pattern in tg't. Observe large oil fires with smoke collums (sic) up to 15,000 feet. Flak was intense and accurate—being in "boxes." Very close. Alt. 26,000 ft. 48 below zero. 0745.**

That mission, my last, came on the day elements of the Third Army broke through to end the siege of Bastogne.

It could well have proved to be my last day alive. Flak at the target hit 13 of our planes, but that was nothing compared to the perils caused by weather. Dick Mabie, now our first pilot, Al Hall, Wolf, Block and I made up the nucleus of a bastard crew, and while waiting for a green light that morning we bet each other that we'd never get off the ground. Our little tower had almost dissolved in the low cloud and mist.

Group had assigned the 414th to Dog Box, the last to take off, and we had been posted to Fox position, almost the last plane. When the tower finally glowed green we climbed in our aircraft, but seemed to sit forever, running up the engines and waiting for our takeoff position. Then as we taxied around the perimeter track we could see the mist swallow each plane moving down the runway.

As its wheels left the strip our plane entered a sea of gray, so Dick climbed straight out for a couple of minutes instead of turning immediately. We expected to break through the leaden mantle momentarily, but it stuck with us on our swing back over the base. Vague light in the radio room abruptly turned darker for a moment as an obscure shape passed over us. Another plane, of course, its pilot feeling his way in a lethal version of "blind man's buff." On the interphone we could hear the bombardier's favorite expletive.

Finally we broke out into a world as silvery brilliant as the other had been dull. Searching the skies for our squadron and group to tie onto, we discovered that we flew alone. Dick circled again, still climbing, and asked us what we wanted to do. We voted loudly and unanimously to go on and find the group if possible. Several wings had briefed for the Silesian oil targets that day, and we hoped to find our outfit over the Dalmatian Coast where the groups had been ordered to take their assigned slots.

Dick turned up the power on the way to Split, hoping to catch the rest of the 97th. Once over the Slavic coast we counted perhaps a dozen groups, circling or sailing serenely off to the north, but none was ours. So we started our own track, parallel to this apparently endless stream. Ten pairs of eyes searched for B17 tails bearing our group markings as we passed one formation after another. Finally, about even with Budapest, we saw it: a group at our assigned altitude, cruising without a fourth squadron.

We slid into the rear slot position in Charlie Box, wondering what had become of the 414th. We barely had time to get adjusted when the group turned into the IP at Odertal. During the bomb run flak damaged several planes in our box, and as each one dropped behind, Dick moved up to fill a blank position. By the time our bomb doors closed we flew in Baker slot, just off the squadron leader's right wing.

When we returned to Amendola, clouds and rain had cleared away, and no more exuberant crew ever drank its shots of rye whisky and crowded around the interrogation officer. We all grinned stupidly but proudly when we learned that the rest of the squadron had given up that morning in their efforts to form up. Most of the 414th's planes had landed at other fields which reported better visibility.

I popped the cork on my champagne before evening chow. Despite its dreadful taste, Flood, Grove, Tuk and I drained every drop from that celebration bottle. I had cause for extra ritual. Because of the double credit policy my mission count came to 51.

Italy
Dec. 26,

Well, you can throw away your horseshoe now. I flew my last mission today. I wanted to surprise you so haven't mentioned all the trips or the number. . . Yeah man! 50 + 1 for the record. Really sweated this last one too. One hard day's work. Just 5 months to the day since I flew the first one.

It's hard to say what things happen next,

but don't get too anxious about anything for a
month yet at least. . .

> *Boy, I can't tell you how much I'm relieved*
to know I don't have to go thru that again. Just
like you feel when you've been going to a dentist
for a long time and finally know you're thru. . .

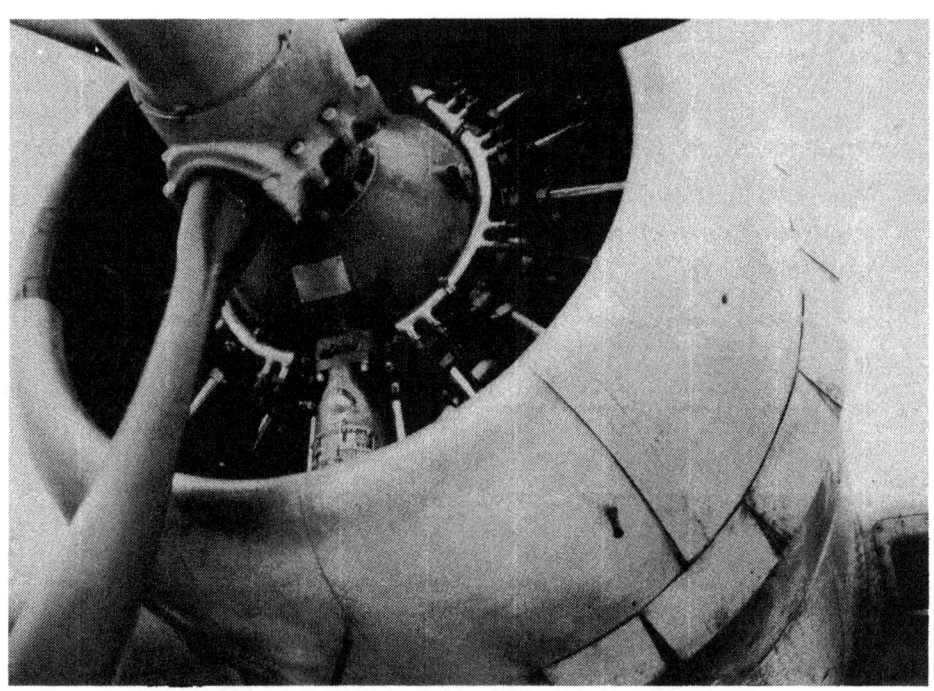

1200 h.p. Wright Cyclone engine, cowl flaps partly open.

32. Going Home

Much had happened in those five months of missions, not only in our crew but in the entire war against Germany. The decision to concentrate the air effort toward crippling Jerry's oil supplies had been effective. By the end of January, 1945, 17 of 36 refineries still in German hands had stopped producing, and nearly all the rest could turn out very little. As late as December the main allied bombing objective was to shut off the 11 synthetic plants which produced 70 percent of Hitler's small remaining aviation and motor fuel supply.

A shortage of fuel had been a major factor in the collapse of Jerry's Ardennes offensive in December. Then in January, 1945, the Wehrmacht massed between 1200 and 1500 tanks to try to halt a Russian offensive in upper Silesia. The German command, however, couldn't make proper use of its armor because of a lack of fuel. On Jan. 19, Albert Speer, Germany's production boss, sent a secret report to Hitler to show that December production of aviation fuel should have been 107,000 tons, but totaled only 25,000 tons.

In addition, allied bombing of transportation targets had brought German industry near a point of collapse. Between August and December in 1944, monthly coal shipments by both rail and water fell from 7.4 to 2.7 million tons. After the war, military analyst B.H. Liddell Hart wrote that allied air forces had made possible the successful invasion of Normandy, then had opened the way for breakout and victory.

Back in 1941 the United States Army Air Forces had listed few operational air groups and reported about 9,000 pilots in schools. By the end of 1944 the U.S. had 41,600 planes at home and 31,100 overseas. Even by the end of 1944 it had graduated 226,000 pilots. The Air Forces had 1,100,000 officers and men overseas.

Success in the air over Europe had not come easily and without cost. The combined losses of British and American airmen from Sept. 3, 1939, to VE Day far exceeded the dead in combined British and American land forces from the invasion of Normandy to the end of the war. British and American bomber losses alone totaled more than 20,000 planes. Britain had lost 79,281 airmen and the U.S. 19,265. Even by Nov. 30, 1944, the U.S. air casualty lists, including missing and wounded, totaled 104,818 men. German losses had been even higher.

By the end of the European war, after 19 months of operations, the 15th Air Force alone had destroyed about half of all the fuel production capacity of Europe. It had aimed 303,842 tons of bombs at targets in 12 countries. The 15th had flown 148,955 individual bomber sorties and 87,732 fighter sorties.

Our outfit, the 97th, had a steady and effective hand in all of it. A mission to Regensburg on Dec. 9, 1944, had made it the first U.S. heavy bomber group to complete 400 missions. The group also received its second Distinguished Unit Citation, this time for our blasting of the Romana-Americana refinery at Ploesti on Aug. 18.

After I left it the 97th continued its distinguished record of missions, including the first against Berlin from the south on March 24, 1945, a 1,500-mile round trip to visit a Daimler-Benz tank engine plant. Its final combat effort, on April 26, 1945, made it the first heavy bomber group to fly 483 combat missions. The group had dropped 26,666 tons of bombs on enemy targets.

More than 6,000 men flew combat missions with the 97th during the war, and the group lost 724 air crewmen, killed or missing in action, one of the lowest ratios of combat losses in the European theater. In 33 months the group lost 114 aircraft while flying 12,934 sorties by individual planes. One of its planes, in September, 1943, became the first heavy bomber to fly 100 missions. Nineteen of the group's planes later equalled that record.

Air crews of the 97th flew some of its planes back to the States in the summer of 1945. Others flew B17s to Germany to be scrapped. Some of the airplanes sat in desert storage in Arizona for years until they were broken up for scrap. The Army Air Forces deactivated the group's squadrons on Oct. 29, 1945, but the 97th later was commissioned as an Air Force heavy bomber wing. Flying B52s, the 97th Wing was finally decommissioned Jan. 1, 1992, in Arkansas.

Anglo-American air forces had dropped more than 1.2 million tons of bombs on Germany during the war, 72 percent of them after July 1, 1944. The shameful element of all that bomb-dropping was the 39 percent that were directed at cities and towns, compared to only about 14.5 percent at oil targets.

Behind this was the British Bomber Command's area bombing policy, pursued relentlessly by Air Marshal Sir Arthur T. Harris. In contrast with the U.S. strategic operation against military targets, Harris wanted to break the morale of German civilians. His policy didn't work, as proved by studies after the war, but instead diverted men, money and equipment ineffectively. The U.S. Strategic Bombing Survey after the shooting ended showed that area bombing had a negligible effect on total German production. Instead, it was a major cause of the deaths of about 635,000 civilians in the greater Reich. The only USAF area bombing had been at Hamburg in July and August of 1943 and at Dresden Feb. 13 and 15, 1945.

So far as we could tell, our own missions could have killed civilians only if they were engaged in war production and had remained in the target area. Our crew's participation had added a mere fragment in the jigsaw puzzle of victory, and my own contribution had been even more minute. But at the end of 1944 I allowed myself temporarily to savor a reasonable slice of credit. Of my 30 missions (which added up to 51 in the official count), 17 had been to oil targets, seven against transportation, two against aircraft plants, two to tactical targets, one against a munitions plant, and one against submarines. In retrospect, I rated my toughest targets in this order: Ploesti (four missions), the Silesian refineries (eight missions), and the Vienna area (five missions).

Italy,
Dec. 27,

Just a lazy day here, and do I like it!. . .Just like having a ticket, being all packed, and waiting for transportation. Sure a swell feeling to have.

Italy,
Dec. 28,

What a life this is. . . Am taking time to get

acquainted around here now. Just sit and talk to
guys--sweat out mail call, and chow. . .
     Hall finished today. Dick is the only one left
in the old crew. He has 44 now. I doubt if I'll get to
go home with any of my crew. . . Lots of red tape
to go thru between now and then. . .

At this time those of us who had finished mostly
gave our attention to simple, inconsequential events. Posting of the next day's mission roster, which formerly raised a
stir in our tent, now barely ruffled an eybrow. The first
sound of our planes returning from a mission, always a
source of interest in the squadron, now became a casual in-
terruption in a lazy afternoon. Sweeping out the tent or
pausing to visit idly about the weather now moved higher
on a scale of priorities. Our brains had found ways to cut
the throttles back.

                                Italy
                                Dec. 30,
                                Sat. nite.

     Well, I'm all alone in the old tent now. Ed,
Tuk and Grove left this morning with a lot of other
guys who have finished. . .
     Still rainy and cold here. . .
     I hope to catch the next shipment out of
here. Not as easy and as fast as it was coming over.
Guess they think they can take their time about me
from now on. . .

The processing of papers seemed to take two or
three weeks before crewmen could ship out for home, and

we couldn't escape the feeling that having wrung every bit of use from us the Army had set us aside.

Italy,
Dec. 31, '44

Pay day, and the last day of 1944. . . It's snowing. . . pretty hard. . .
Am sitting right beside the stove, and one side of me is chilly, and the other is about broiled. .

Italy,
Jan. 1, 1945
5 p.m.

. . .Turned in my flying equipment. . . Am trying to get my clothes in shape. . .using carbon tet to take the soot off my ODs. . .

In giving up my flying gear one tiny matter still needed attention. People in Army supply jobs always seemed to wear the newest and best uniforms. So I feared that, without some careful planning, someone in our crew supply shack would get his hands on my nearly new leather flying jacket. In the mess tent one day a ground crew chief about my size readily agreed to swap his jacket for mine. His bore all the oil spots and tatters of a useful life. When I turned it in, the supply officer at the line shack stared at the old jacket and at me in obvious disbelief. He was powerless to challenge me and knew that I had simply found a method to thwart the "Army way."

Italy

Jan. 3, '45

    . . . A new crew came in yesterday, so 4 of them moved in with me. Just about all settled now, so it's nearly the same as it was before my bunch left. . .

Italy
Jan. 4,

    Don't write any more letters to me. I wouldn't get them anyway. . .
    Expect to leave this area in a couple days. . .
    Sure feels swell to know I'll be coming home soon. Can hardly wait till I see the old Yewnited States and home. . .

Italy
Jan. 6, '45

    Well, I spent nearly all day yesterday packing and getting ready to leave, and now they say we are delayed another day. . .
    I don't know how I'm going to take that 15-below-zero weather. The dampness here makes it seem almost that cold tho. . .

In a solemn ceremony befitting its importance, I passed my overshoes on to the radio operator who had moved into my tent along with three others in his crew. After spending a final night in it I also left him my eiderdown sack liner. These men hadn't flown a mission yet and seemed to be awed by my old-timer status. They asked and

261

got my advice on how to temper the cold of high altitude, then my hope that they'd be more successful at it than I.

Finally, I said goodby to folks at group and squadron operations whom I had worked with--and still knew. Many faces had changed in the past month.

About 20 of us homeward-bound types crowded ourselves and all we owned into a jukin' ship on Jan. 7 for a short ride to Pamigliano airfield near Naples. We wanted to enjoy this last flight in Italy, but our pilot wouldn't let us. He had little experience, apparently, and for some reason buzzed the Pamigliano field once before making a standard approach. As he made his final turn toward the field, a couple of pilots in our crowd displayed some anxiety. Our novice driver, probably unused to the light ship, touched down more than halfway down the runway. He braked hard, but we went off the end of the strip and sank into the spongy soil, all four propellers whipping mud in the air.

Dejected and disgusted, we threw our bags through the hatches and slid out. Almost immediately, a base crew arrived and soon began digging, but we sat there for nearly three hours before somebody thought of sending a truck to take us to town. As we left the hapless aircraft, two tracked tugs strained without effect on cables attached to the wheel struts.

The truck delivered us at our objective, the Caserma, after dark and after all signs of evening chow had vanished. A listless non-com led us through the 15th century stone fort to a long barracks room. At the far end a shuttered window overlooked the Bay of Naples. We hadn't eaten since morning, so several of us rousted a cook, who protested loudly to our demands but eventually surrendered half a case of canned peaches. Next we found mattress covers and the usual pile of straw for padding hard wooden bunks, making it possible finally for us to get some sleep.

Cold, spare quarters in the best circumstances, the Caserma in January, 1945, extended little in our behalf beyond its exceptional view of the bay. This typical Army replacement depot now housed hundreds of soldiers awaiting ships that would take them home. About nine out of ten men in the depot at that time came from the 34th Infantry Division, which had landed in North Africa late in 1942.

We couldn't find heat anywhere except in the kitchen, and spent most of our hours trying to keep warm. Someone produced a football which occupied our feeble talents for several days, our awkward attempts to run and pass succeeding despite uneven paving stones and restrictive Army overcoats.

My last letter home from Italy went into the mail on the day U.S. troops invaded the island of Luzon in the Philippines.

Italy
Jan. 9,

Things are progressing slowly but surely towards that day when I can leave this place and come home. We are living in regular billets now. . .
We can see a show almost every night. . .
We can also play football, etc. . .

The cold had settled in, and it snowed one day. I'll always remember Mt. Vesuvius as it appeared then, erupting during a snowstorm.

Finally, a major in transportation command came through our quarters one day and said we'd board ship the next morning. He warned us against trying to take home any "contraband," including weapons. His words took their desired effect, at least on me. After he departed, the little Beretta pistol I had bought at Amendola came out of my barracks bag and within minutes a man in the next bunk bought it for $25. It had no special meaning even as a keepsake, so I didn't feel cheated when the Army let us board our ship without a search.

Even after more than a year of repair, Naples harbor remained quite a mess, and engineers had even put sunken ships to use as rudimentary docks. Our assigned vessel couldn't pull close to shore, so to get aboard we carried our bags a hundred yards or so over water, balancing on planks that were mounted on floats. The single, olive drab line of soldiers required several hours to fill the waiting ship. Each of us carried a card indicating a berthing space, and patient sailors showed us the way.

We had boarded the Army troop transport "West Point," which had been launched in 1940 as the liner "America." Four of us who had been in air units settled into a compartment with about 50 infantrymen. Two propeller shaft housings divided our space in the stern into three sections, connected by flights of steel steps which bridged the housings. Each open section held about 20 of us and provided triple tiers of canvas cots mounted in pipe frames. One latrine in the middle section served the entire compartment, but only its john proved useful. After the first day we gave up trying to wash much in the salt water.

Our ship left the harbor late in the evening on Jan. 16. Its inmates began a schedule that was dictated largely by the enormous task of feeding more than 1,100 men, twice a day. Chow lines started forming in companionways at about 7 a.m. and continued until about 10:30 a.m. They formed again from about 3 p.m. to 6 p.m. In those lines we collected masses of sticky preparations spooned into our trays from steam tables and ate them while standing at chest-high boards.

This arrangement worked satisfactorily for the day and a half that we moved sedately through the Mediterranean. Once we passed the Gibraltar Straits and a whooping destroyer escort, however, we dipped into deep swells from the Atlantic and our woes began. Those of us who had been flying scarcely felt this gentle rise and fall, but nearly all of our bunk mates from the "Red Bull" Division turned green. Most buried themselves in their cots, and except for frantic dashes to the latrine, strayed little for the rest of our trip.

We had made some good friends among these men and felt their wretchedness. Then we discovered that about a dozen of us who could still stand would have to clean up every two or three hours, and not the latrines alone, but every vomit-covered aisle. We lost the last of our compassion while mopping those redolent decks, and as a labor saver we begged the ship's crew to lend us buckets, which we left near the sickest in our compartment. Poker games, which had started while we sat in Naples harbor, dwindled to nothing, and chow lines shortened dramatically. It was a pity that the food was so bad because we could have had all we wanted.

On the first afternoon on the Atlantic several of us, seeking refuge from our smelly quarters, lay on deck under a gun mount near the stern. The sun warmed us to a listless state and we hadn't paid much attention as whistles blew and sailors dashed about their business. Then the gun above us went off and we jumped about a foot. The captain had ordered anti-aircraft drill. Our ears still ringing, we scrambled into the open to watch Navy gunners as they tried to hit a parachute flare hanging two or three miles above the stern. None of the gun crews came close, and we told the crew at the gun near us that if the Germans had been that bad the war would be over.

That night our ship headed directly north. In line for chow next morning we could see ice on every exposed inch on deck. Waves broke above the height of the ship, which soon traded its roll for a twisting climb and then a shuddering dive. The shudder came from propellers as their blades rose out of the sea during each downward move. In our compartment, propeller shafts transmitted this vibration to our bones through floors and bulkheads. Sack-bound ground troops hugged the pipes of their bunks and turned gray.

Every surface, even ship's antennas, carried several inches of ice on Jan. 25 as tugs pushed us next to a covered wharf in Boston harbor. Lines of weary but thankful troops carried their bags down gangways that led directly to a train. On the coaches, Red Cross women handed each of us a glass of the best milk anyone could remember.

Within an hour or two we unloaded again in fresh snow and bitter cold at Camp Miles Standish, where we remained for three days while the Army sorted us out for further transportation. I delighted in my first shower and shave since leaving Amendola, and in the mess halls we stuffed ourselves with fresh meat and vegetables, butter and milk. I sent this telegram to my folks:

534PM JAN 26 1945

MRS DWIGHT C BOTTS

LUDDEN NDAK

DEAR MOM YOUR PRODIGAL SON HAS RETURNED
WELL AND HAPPY. HOME SOON. LOVE.

JACK

On the 28th a whole trainload of infantrymen and a few of us airmen left Boston, bound for Ft. Snelling. The 34th Division men had come largely from Minnesota, Iowa and the Dakotas, so it made sense to route us through Minneapolis. We rode old coaches instead of troop cars and were moving in the right direction, so we couldn't complain much. On our arrival on the 30th, the Minneapolis newspapers gave us a big spread, including photos and interviews. I hurried into town immediately and spent the whole evening in luxury, soaking in a hotel bathtub.

Next day a Soo Line train gave me an agonizingly slow ride to Oakes. From there a telephone call alerted my parents in Ludden and, waiting for them to arrive, I had my first good haircut in months.

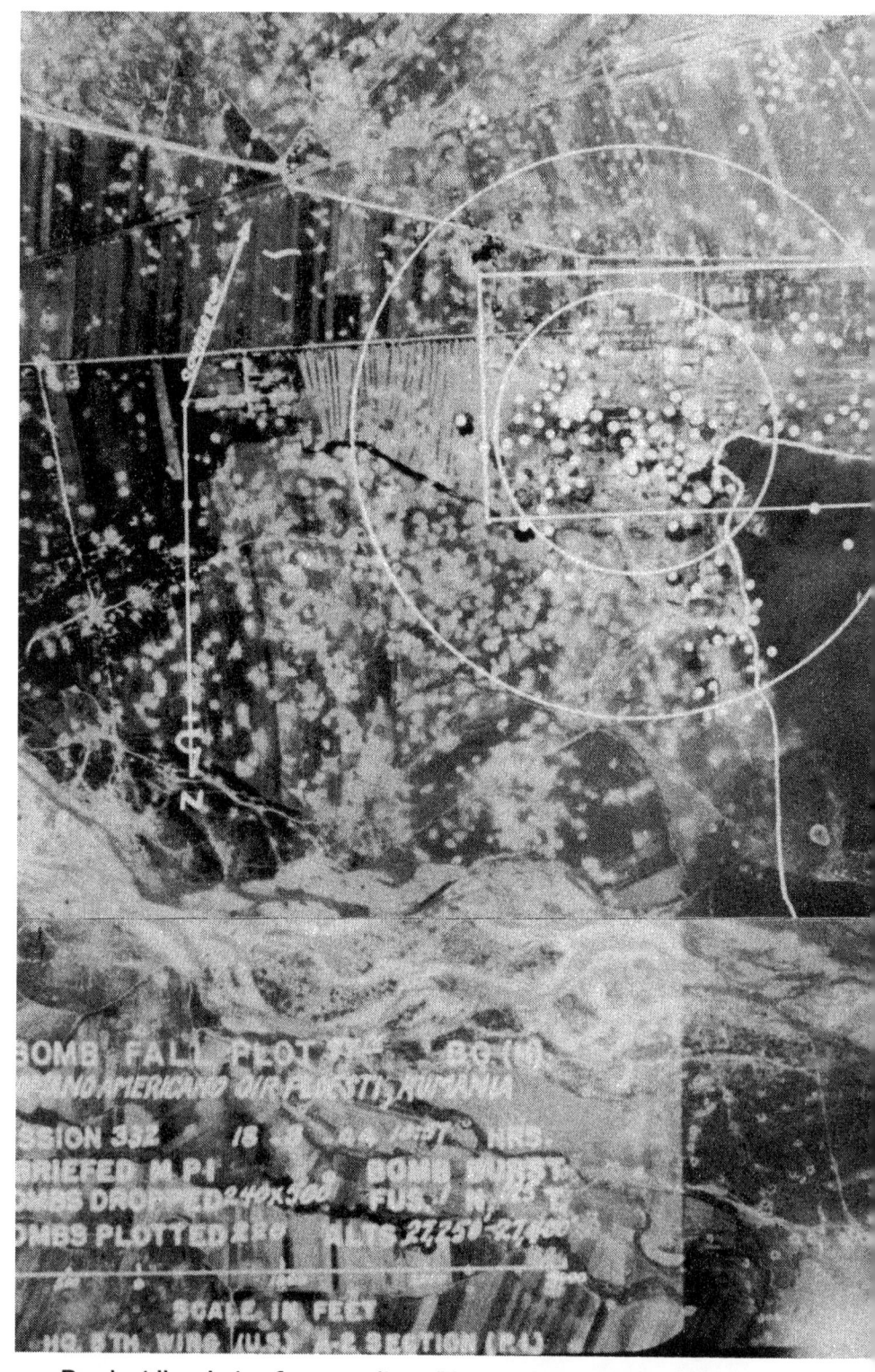

Bomb-strike photo of our results at Ploesti's Romano-Americano
oil refinery on Aug. 18, 1944. The mission won the 97th a unit citation.

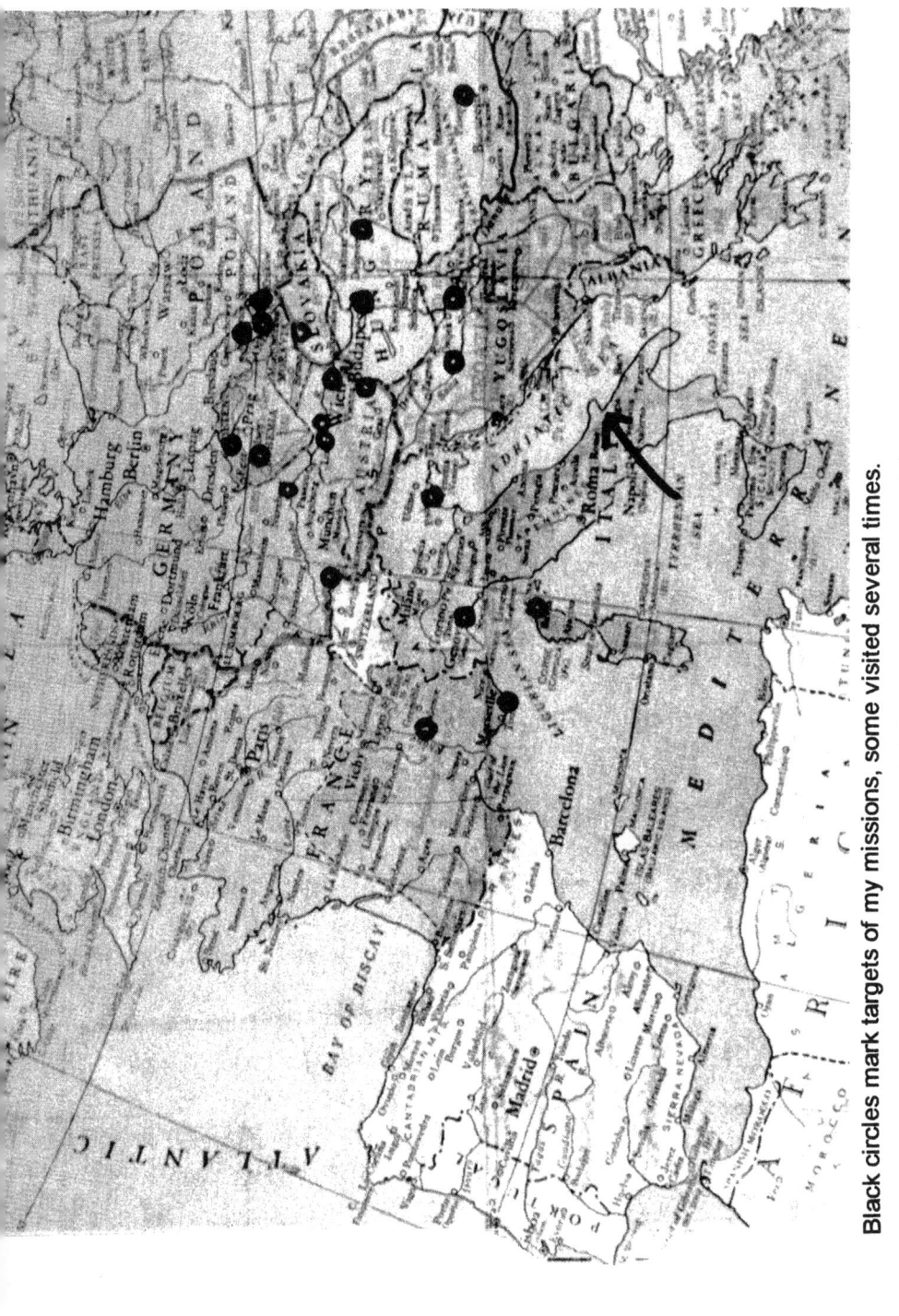

Black circles mark targets of my missions, some visited several times.

33. Me? An Instructor?

Twenty three days at home, even in a North Dakota winter, can overcome even the worst case of combat fatigue. I felt great, but still eagerly accepted all the steaks, milk and fresh fruit we could find. Just sitting, visiting and wallowing in comfortable surroundings satisfied most of my needs, however, and simple things like a bed, a chair, clean clothes and real plates on a table fascinated me for days. More gratification came in a regular movie theater, in Oakes, which didn't require pauses for rewinding the film.

At home we talked about the war a little, but mostly we enjoyed each other. My overseas service had been compressed into six months, and my parents hadn't changed much since my June visit. Perhaps I had, but our health and an assurance of continuity contributed most to our contentment. Though we had little information about my brother's assignment in the Pacific, his worst problems very likely were heat, lack of sanitation and a shortage of good food.

Four regiments of Marines, meanwhile, landed on Iwo Jima on Feb. 19.

Few of my old friends were around to help celebrate my return. Military service had enrolled most of them and some of the rest were at college. My photo album grew in size with pictures taken in Italy, in what already seemed another lifetime. My mother cleaned and pressed uniforms and even sewed my T. Sgt. stripes to my sleeves.

Then, the allotment of furlough days having passed, the Army summoned me back. Army air crewmen like me who had completed one tour of duty reported to centers set up to evaluate and reassign them. I arrived on Feb. 26 at such a base at Santa Ana, Calif., where thousands waited for new jobs. Nine days there became memorable only because of the delights of Los Angeles and Hollywood, where any GI fresh from duty overseas had only to name his desires. All of us had passes to leave the base after morning roll call each day, and special mess hall rations filled us with every goody one could imagine.

Each of us stood and sat for hours of medical and psychiatric exams, and during one of them a gray-haired Lt. Colonel asked me if I'd welcome a few additional weeks of rest and recreation. It sounded great to me. So two days later, on March 6, a handful of us started by train to a convalescent hospital at Ft. George Wright in Spokane, Wash. The Army had decided to pamper me some more and to delay my reassignment to duty.

On March 7, a day we spent in Portland, Ore., 9th Armored Division troops captured a railroad bridge over the Rhine River at Remagen, Germany.

Five weeks in Spokane convinced me again that one probably should accept good offers as they appear. Whatever the Army's reason for this delightful reward in the great Northwest, I extracted every benefit. "Convalescents," infantryman to airman, soaked up sun and calories by day and passable Washington beer by night. Workshops allowed us to occupy our minds and hands while we relaxed, so I checked into a radio shop and started making a receiver.

News reports of our forces pouring in masses across the northern Rhine came to several of us on March 24 as we worked on our little radios. After completing the receiver, I switched to a wood shop, made a cabinet for it and sent it home to North Dakota. For recreation on the hospital grounds we rode horses through the woods, and crewmen who had been in England, Italy and in the Pacific swapped war stories for hours.

Several of us were playing basketball in the gym on April 12 when we heard the news that President Roosevelt had died of a stroke at Warm Springs, Ga.

Then announcements from Europe started coming in clusters. We learned of Hitler's suicide on May 1, and of the surrender of the German high command on the 7th.

Inevitably my idyl had to end, and because the war continued in the Pacific the Army thought it still needed my help. My reassignment orders dispatched me back to the Air Forces Training Command, this time as an "instructor" at a flight radio school at Truax Field, Madison, Wis. About 20 of us who had completed combat tours in bombers learned of our new teaching careers abruptly on our arrival at Truax on June 2. The assignment stunned all of us. I doubt that anybody appreciated assignment as an instructor, in our case because we thought that the war was about over, and especially because we would be thrust again into the nonsense of the Training Command.

On my first day at Truax a first sergeant chewed on me for not switching my 15th Air Force patch to my right shoulder. Then a second looey, even more pink-faced than most, created a scene when I failed to salute as he passed in a Jeep. This clearly wouldn't do.

All of us who had come down from Spokane still had two weeks of accumulated furlough coming so we went home to think over our new posting. During those weeks at home a letter arrived from Skok who reported that Jerry Milburn, missing since the past July, had been declared dead. Phil's letter added news that Dolton apparently had survived bailing out in November.

Back in Madison on June 23 about a dozen of us who were to be instructors agreed that we'd look for some other assignment. For one thing, I couldn't see myself, a 20-year-old "veteran," instructing new radio students, most of whom were in their thirties at that time. We inquired at base headquarters and learned that we could enter navigation training in the Air Transport Command. Several of us jumped at the chance and signed waivers in which we agreed to be sent into combat areas again if necessary. We knew enough about the ATC to suppress any concerns about being shot at. Some of us might have welcomed a few stray bullets over some of the chicken details we had seen at Truax.

We seemed to wait forever, but finally, on July 14 about 40 of us who had been radio operators in bombers arrived at the Reno, Nev., Army Air Base for operational training as radio/navigators. The Air Transport Command had switched to LORAN navigation, which ended the need for traditionally trained navigators in their crews. At Reno we would learn to navigate with LORAN and would be taught enough dead reckoning to back it up. When we graduated by the end of August the ATC would assign each of us to a crew flying regularly across the Pacific, mostly on hospital evacuation planes.

Our classes started immediately and most of us en-joyed the training, especially the new electronics. We learned what we needed to know about map reading, pilotage and dead reckoning. We added a refresher on radio navigation, then switched to LORAN, which fascinated everybody.

The letters stand for Long Range Navigation, and the technique is based on the time a radio signal requires to travel between two points. To learn his position, an operator on a plane would tune in a pair of LORAN sending stations, which usually operated on coastlines. He fed the signals, a short, repeated "dit," into a receiver which displayed them as two blips on a cathode ray tube. He then measured the time difference between the blips in microseconds. Next he tuned in another pair of senders and recorded the time difference between those.

The operator/navigator found the puzzle's key in a LORAN map, which displayed time differences in hundreds of lines. The time difference between two stations would be the same anywhere on one of the lines. The operator had only to find the two lines which represented the two readings he had recorded, and the spot where those two lines crossed on the map represented his position at the time of his readings. Since its development during World War II, LORAN has remained the basic international navigation system, but has been teamed with computers and satellites to calculate positions automatically.

We studied the theory and equipment in classrooms for half of each day, then flew in groups of about eight at a time for practice with the equipment in the air. Although the transport command normally flew four-engine Douglas C54s in its trans-ocean flights, at Reno we flew in two-engine Curtiss C46s, which didn't impress us much. Our classes included operators who had flown in B17s, B24s, B29s, B25s and B26s, and universally, despite our combat experience, we cringed at every takeoff and landing in the "flying whales." With flaps down, especially, they tended to swing from side to side, their tails oscillating wildly. The stable B17 and its snug radio room now became one of my prized memories.

The base at Reno had been built in a natural, shallow bowl high on a shelf in the Sierra foothills. Lights extending from each runway ran up these hills, and at night made the field appear suspended in a sparkling spider web. Takeoffs and landings, day or night, gave one the feeling of sliding up and down the hillsides. Flying in an oscillating airplane only added to our tension.

Passes to Reno amounted to a wild adventure because one could lose touch with reality in the town's bars and gambling casinos, which never closed. GIs from the air base won or lost many thousands in a day. Buses carried airmen to and from the base at all hours, mostly because nobody could find a bed in town. Those who insisted on staying overnight usually could beg a blanket and floor space at a house kept by the Navy Mothers Club.

Then came the atomic bombing of Hiroshima and Nagasaki, and on Aug. 14, shortly before our classes ended, Japan accepted Allied surrender terms. Several of us learned about the end of the war while flying near the Grand Canyon. The plane's engineer heard the news flash on the radio and, not thinking of the consequences, punched the plane's bail-out buzzer. We trainees, who lay half asleep in the garage-size cargo space, reacted as combat veterans should. I had one of the side hatches removed and one leg though it when the joker came through the bulkhead door, screaming for us to stay put. Exuberance had nearly spoiled a happy event.

We all celebrated in the next few days and completed our classes as scheduled, but not surprisingly the Air Transport Command decided that it now had enough radio/navigators. Those of us at Reno and millions of other GIs around the world became redundant overnight and started thinking about getting back to civilian life. The War Department, facing a massive mound of processing, had set up a discharge system to provide some order. Under these rules, a serviceman would base his discharge eligibility on points, one for every month of service, one more for every month overseas, five for each battle star and five for each decoration. For early discharge, one had to have 85 points. Those servicemen with 84 points would be eligible next, and so forth.

By Sept. 1 my points totaled 85, but the Army Air Forces now began to feel the effects of having operated like a separate service throughout the war. All indications pointed toward formation of a new air arm as soon as possible, but for now the Army announced that it would discharge its own men, which didn't include air units. A fit of pique, perhaps, but we could understand it. The Reno base commander told us that we'd have to wait until the air forces set up their own discharge centers.

That might take a while, so a hundred or so of us who considered ourselves civilians being held against our will looked about for pleasant activity. For about a week several of us regularly rode through the Sierra foothills on Army horses that had been supplied by a remount station. Then three of us discovered two L5s, small Stinson observation planes which had been used mostly for the pleasure of transport pilots at the Reno base. A staff sergeant we met at a bar in town said he could check us out in the planes and we could fly them.

On the first day all three of us checked out and soloed, afterwards buzzing around northwest Nevada as we wished. That lasted about a week before a major on the flight line discovered our sport and plucked our feathers. He could have brought military charges but, aware of our short-time status, simply enjoined further use of government property. He suggested that we indulge our flying whims at a civilian field.

That possibility hadn't occurred to us. A little inquiry led us to the Sky Ranch, a barren strip cut from sand and sagebrush north of Sparks, Nev., east of Reno. There we learned that we could check out for student certificates, then rent light 85 h.p. Aeroncas for $5 an hour. All three of us had to undergo physical exams before receiving civilian licenses, but no matter, we had found a way to spend our remaining days in the Army.

At the Sky Ranch friendly pilots and managers allowed us to do almost as we wished, and once we satisfied them that we wouldn't pile up their Aeroncas we tried everything. The manager knew we had passed navigational courses, so although we held only CAA student certificates, he let us fly as far as a load of fuel would take us.

This almost-daily flying continued until Oct. 11, my 21st birthday. I returned to the base from Reno at about 4 p.m. and was told to pack up. Orders had come for me to escort five others by train to Great Falls, Mont., where the Army Air Forces would process our discharges. The five who were supposed to be in my care had left already for the depot in town, and a WAC Jeep driver stood by impatiently as my belongings went into bags. I clung desperately to the vehicle's seat during the dash down the mountain and arrived at the depot only minutes before the train pulled out.

My transportation orders specified that all six of us were to have first class accommodations, which meant we'd get Pullman berths that night. But a conductor informed me without blinking that all the berths had been taken. My only thoughts were that the government obviously had paid for our berths and we were being cheated out of them on our last days in the Army. Frustrated, I went into the car's smoker where I complained loudly to a man who wore a railroad uniform. Within minutes, all six of us had our berths. The railroader in the smoker happened to be a senior conductor, dead-heading home. He read the riot act to our train conductor, who apparently had sold our berths to six other people and had pocketed the cash.

At the Great Falls base it took three days of standing in processing lines and supply queues for me to give up my extra uniforms and my attachment to the Army. A desk-dweller in one line offered me a permanent rank as buck sergeant if I'd sign over for another hitch. I never answered his invitation and he never pressed it.

At 2:30 p.m. on Oct. 17, 1945, I regained my rank as civilian, first class, six days after turning 21. With the discharge document came a brass eagle lapel pin, or "Ruptured Duck," and another train ticket, this time to carry me home.

Epilogue

I revisited Amendola, Italy, 46 years later with my wife Dorris during a European vacation. We expected to find little more than plowed ground and few traces of the old strips and the bivouac area.

We dismounted from a bus at the gates of a major Italian air base, a permanent installation complete with palm trees in its landscaping. Across the present four-lane highway to the north, where our tents once flapped in the wind, a small but modern community houses the base's officers.

At a gas station on the highway I found a couple of sheets of steel matting, obviously from the old World War II strips, being used in 1990 for parking cars during oil changes.

Bibliography

Arnold, Henry H., *Global Mission,* New York, Harper & Brothers, 1949.

Bartz, Karl, *Swastika in the Air,* London, William Kimber, 1956.

Bidinian, Larry, *The Combined Allied Bombing Offensive Against the German Civilians, 1942-1945,* Coronado Press, 1976.

Combat Squadrons of the Air Force; World War II, Washington, D.C. Gov't Printing Office, 1969.

Commager, Henry Steele, *The Story of the Second World War,* Boston; Little, Brown, 1945.

Cook, Ronald and Nesbit, Roy C., *Target: Hitler's Oil,* London, William Kimber, 1985.

Craven, W.F. and Cate, J.L., *The Army Air Forces in World War II,* 3 vols., Chicago, University of Chicago Press. 1947-51.

Cubbins, William R., *The War of The Cottontails,* Chapel Hill, N.C., Algonquin, 1989.

Dugan, James and Stewart, Carroll, *Ploesti,* New York, Random House, 1962.

Francis, Devon, *Flak Bait,* Washington, D.C., Zenger, 1948.

Frankland, Noble, *Bomber Offensive, The Devastation of Europe,* Ballantine, 1970.

Freeman, Roger A., *The Mighty Eighth.* A History of the 8th U.S. Army Air Force, New York, Doubleday, 1970.

Freeman, Roger A., *B-17 Fortress at War*, New York, Charles Scribner's, Sons, 1977.

Green, William, *Famous Bombers of the Second World War*, Garden City, N.Y., Hanover House, 1959.

Green, Constance M., Thomson, Harry C., Roots, Peter C. and Mayo, Lida, *The Ordnance Dept.:* Planning Munitions for War, Washington, D.C., Dept. of Army, 1955.

Gurney, Maj. Gene, *The War in the Air*, New York, Crown, 1962.

Infield, Glenn, *Big Week*, New York, Brassey's, 1993.

Jablonski, Edward, *Flying Fortress*, Garden City, N.Y., Doubleday, 1965.

Jablonski, Edward, *Airwar*, 2 vols., Garden City, N.Y., Doubleday, 1971.

Middlebrook, Martin, *The Berlin Raids*, London, Viking, 1988.

Morrison, Wilbur H., *Fortress Without a Roof*, New York, St. Martin's Press, 1982.

Nalty, Bernard C. and Berger, Carl, *The Men Who Bombed The Reich*, New York, Elsevier-Dutton, 1978.

Newby, Leroy W., *Into the Guns of Ploesti*, Osceoloa, Wis., Motorbooks International, 1991.

Pilot's Flight Operating Instructions for Army Models B17F and G. AN 01-20EF-1; A.P. No. 2099C.

Radio Operator's Information File, U.S. Army Air Forces, 1945.

Rust, Kenn C., *15th Air Force Story*, Temple City, Calif., Historical Aviation Album, 1976.

Rust, Kenn C. *Twelfth Air Force Story*, Temple City, Calif., Historical Aviation Album, 1975.

Stiles, Bert, *Serenade to The Big Bird*, New York, W.W. Norton, 1947.

Target: Germany. The AAF's Official Story of the VIII
    Bomber Command's First Year Over Europe, New
    York, Simon & Schuster, 1943.
U.S. Army in World War II, Chronology 1941-1945,
    Compiled by Mary H. Williams, Washington, D.C.,
    1960.
U.S. Strategic Bombing Survey, Washington, D.C., U.S.
    Government Printing Office, 1946-47.
Webster, Sir Charles and Frankland, Noble, *The Strategic
    Air Offensive Against Germany, 1939 1945,*
    Vol. III Part 5, London, H.M. Stationery Office,
    1961.

Author's Note:

This reprinting was prompted because,
although all copies of the book had been sold,
there was a continuing demand for it,
especially from air war veterans or members of their families.
The interest has been gratifying to the author.

—Jack Botts

0-595-26131-0

CPSIA information can be obtained
at www.ICGtesting.com
Printed in the USA
FSHW010516110319
56253FS